THE COLOUR
OF FOOD
a memoir of life, love & dinner

ANNE ELSE

AWA PRESS

First print edition published in 2014 by Awa Press, Level Three,
11 Vivian Street, Wellington 6011, New Zealand.

ISBN 978-1-927249-15-4

Ebook editions published in 2013
epub ISBN 978-1-877551-92-5
mobi ISBN 978-1-877551-93-2

A catalogue record for this book is available from
the National Library of New Zealand.

Cover design by Pieta Brenton
Typesetting by Tina Delceg
This book is typeset in Sabon
Printed by Midas Printing International Ltd, China

Find more great books at awapress.com.

THE COLOUR OF FOOD

'As with all life stories, the individual details make it extraordinary – and in Anne Else's case the details are more extraordinary than many'
Ruth Nichol, *New Zealand Books*

'She has the writer's instinct for a good story and the editor's keen eye for accuracy and brevity…This is a disarmingly intimate life account that fast forwards and winds back as she savours and suffers a life of friendship, motherhood, love, loss and mealtimes'
Susette Goldsmith, *The Listener*

'I fell in love with the style of this book from the start…it is an absolute delight to read this delicate morsel of a book that leaves a lingering taste of a meal lovingly shared and enjoyed'
Elisabeth Marrow, *The Daily Post*

'Anne Else writes beautifully about food memories, good and bad, and interweaves funny, interesting, and at times sad stories about people in her life. The recipes mentioned are collected at the end, by the time you finish this life-affirming memoir, you'll feel like those recipes have been passed on by an old friend'
Shelley Howells, *Kia Ora*

'The only thing it left me wanting was more. Like a good meal, I just didn't want it to stop. It felt like a real privilege to read such and intimate and honest story'
Sue Kerr, *Five Course Garden* (http://fivecoursegarden.blogspot.co.nz)

'After flicking through just a couple of pages *The Colour of Food* had me hooked…it reads like a novel, but it is real, touching and insightful…an absolute gem'
Nom Nom Panda (http://nomnompanda.blogspot.co.nz)

'I hadn't quite anticipated how [Else] would draw me in with her incredibly vivid storytelling – I ended up reading the whole thing in less than 24 hours…Her experiences are rich and varied, she is open and honest, and the emotions – at both ends of the spectrum – reach out of the book and grab you the whole way through'
Rosa Slack, *The Culinary Explorations of Mrs Cake* (http://www.mrscake.co.nz)

ANNE ELSE is a writer, social commentator, reviewer and food blogger. She has written and edited books on women's writing, adoption, unpaid work, and women's organisations, and her articles and reviews have appeared in many publications, including *New Zealand Listener* and *Landfall*. She has an MA (Hons) in English from the University of Auckland and a PhD from Victoria University of Wellington. In 2004 she was made a Member of the New Zealand Order of Merit for services to literature.

Read Anne's blogs:
Something Else to Eat and *Elsewoman*

Visit Anne on Facebook:
Anne Else Food Memoir

In loving memory of Harvey McQueen,
who shared kitchens, tables and beds
with me for thirty years.

Contents

To start with

I'm three, and I'm sitting in the sun on the grass beside the narrow strip of garden in our long skinny backyard. Before Mum sees me I reach out for a handful of rich dark soil and fill my mouth with its crunchy, crumbly, satisfying warmth.

Now I'm four, watching Mum as she cuts a neat square plug out of an apple. She hides sugar in the hole for me to find and puts back the plug, the cut-lines invisible in the green skin.

When I think about my childhood it's the food I remember most. Apart from that delicious dirt, what I ate was just the standard fare of thousands of 1950s' New Zealand homes, yet I knew how much it mattered. Even more than the Everglaze summer dresses and knitted winter jumpers with matching skirts, food meant pleasure, love and safety. But it could also tip over into revulsion, rejection and danger.

The memories of food go far beyond childhood. Since the day I left home to get married at the age of nineteen, what I have eaten and cooked, and what has been cooked for me, have often seemed to hold the essence of who I thought I was or wanted to be, and how I lived with the people I loved. Food has also been a creative challenge and a daily source of sensual delight.

I haven't tried to cover every aspect of my food experiences over the last sixty years. Instead I have lifted out what seem to me the most interesting and intensely flavoured morsels in the whole complex, many-layered casserole as it has slow-cooked its way through my life. There's a strong emphasis on eating and cooking at home, where food and feelings are always so deeply blended – but home has moved from Auckland to Albania to London to Wellington, with side trips into French territory, real and imagined.

The book doesn't conform strictly to the passing of time. It moves backwards and forwards through the years, so the people I've shared my life with appear at various intervals. For example, Harvey McQueen, my second husband, turns up well before I write about meeting him in 1979.

It's never easy to turn and look intently into your past, then try to bring back what you find there. I hope these ten portions of my life, closely connected but each with its own distinctive character, will be as satisfying for you to read as cooking them up has been for me.

Anne Else

More than enough

It's school holidays and I've spent the morning with Mum while she gets on with the breakfast dishes and the downstairs cleaning, listening to Aunt Daisy, Doctor Paul and Portia Faces Life on the radio, while my little sister plays in the backyard. Just before lunchtime Mum gives me three shillings and I run up the lane and around the corner to Davenport's Bakery for three ninepenny meat pies, hot from the oven. We eat them with soft white bread and butter, and tomato sauce from the red plastic tomato. With only the three of us, there's no need to hurry: Dad won't be home needing his dinner until half past five, and for the time being Mum seems to be on holiday too.

It took me years to recognise that it was my mother who sowed the seeds of the pleasure I get from food. She got profound satisfaction from producing a constant generous supply of meals for herself, her husband and her children. When she was a child, that reliable security had been mostly missing. Many of the stories she told me turned on how hard it had been for her mother, Harriet, to produce any kind of food at all. The stories were like a real-life version of my copy of *Grimm's Fairy Tales*, an old small-print edition of a scary nineteenth-century translation never intended for children. Despite all the bread, cheese, cabbage and sausage in its pages, they were also full of hunger and want, often linked with making a foolish marriage to a stranger.

Harriet did this twice. Her own family was irreproachably respectable. Her father, Arthur, was a well-to-do hardware merchant who had sailed to Gisborne from Ireland in 1867 with his much younger bride, Frances Selina. Frances produced ten children and all of them lived. As my mother told it, Harriet was the youngest and most beautiful of four sisters, but she was painfully shy and sensitive, and when her family started taunting her for being an old maid she vowed she'd let any man have her. At twenty-nine she met Hugo Korth, an exotic Polish exile, who fathered her three children – Rurik, my mother Ryda, and their brother Raymond.

Korth turned out to be a shiftless drunkard. He used to steal vegetables from gardens to feed his family, running home with them at night through the dark streets.

In all the stories about not having enough to eat, someone is running. Harriet leaves her baby in the tent her husband has put up for them to live in, climbs barbed wire fences, and runs across paddocks to get milk from a farmer. She gets her three children to run around the dining table where she sits with one boiled egg, feeding each a small spoonful as they go past, turning it into a game. She borrows threepence from a neighbour and sends Ryda running to the butcher to buy bones for soup.

Harriet had to borrow the threepence because the funeral of her second husband had left her penniless. Korth had brought this man home after meeting him in prison; you would have thought that was warning enough. Mr Steele – he was always 'Mr Steele' in my mother's stories – was handsome and well-educated, and he wooed Harriet by bringing her food for her children.

In 1913 Harriet managed to get a divorce from Korth on the grounds of habitual drunkenness and failure to support, and the next year she married Mr Steele. According to Mum he was a confirmed bachelor who should never have married a mother with children. He became jealous of Harriet's love for them and showed it through food: he would buy good fruit for her and spotted fruit for them.

It didn't take Harriet long to discover that Mr Steele was a con man and a drug addict. As the money disappeared and his gentlemanly act fell apart, she came up with an idea. Sheets were always wearing out down the centre and having to be turned, sides to middle. Why not reinforce the centre with double weaving so the sheets would last longer? She paid a few shillings to protect her patent and the Scottish firm of Findlay's agreed to pay her a royalty of one and a half percent on all 'Backbone' sheeting sold. With the money, she managed to keep her family fed, paying the grocer every three months when she got her cheque.

Eleven years later Mr Steele died. By then it was 1925 and all three children were earning. Harriet couldn't afford to renew her sheeting patent, but she rented a better house and took in lodgers. As far as I know, she and her family never went hungry again.

I first knew my grandmother when I was four. She was seventy-four and living in a rented villa in tiny Avenham Walk in Mount Eden, close enough to our flat for my mother and me to walk to. She had a strange smell, which I realised later came from the raw garlic she grew and ate to keep germs at bay. She would take me for long walks around Mount Eden, stopping every so often to nip cuttings off plants growing over fences and drop them into the woven flax kete she carried everywhere, except when she dressed up to go to town with my mother. When I went home she would wave goodbye to me at her gate with two arms and a raised leg. Although we visited her often, I have no memory of her ever coming to our place for lunch or tea.

I was seven when she managed to buy an old house in Greenhithe, near her youngest son and his family. Most Saturday mornings in summer we would catch the car ferry across the harbour, and my father would drive the long winding metalled roads to take my mother, my sister Susan and me to stay with Grandma for the weekend while he went back and worked overtime building new grocery stores.

The food we ate at Grandma's was different from that at home, and some of it was awful: pale green, slimy, tasteless chokos, and strangely smooth, flabby, damp little cakes she baked in her small green electric stove to save heating up the big black wood-burning one. I dreaded having to use her forks because there were often tiny bits of dried food stuck to the tines. Her eyesight was failing, the washing-up water wasn't hot enough, and the lump of Sunlight soap in the wire soap shaker didn't help much.

As I grew older I lay for hours under the plum tree on the palm-frond mat Grandma had brought back from her flying-boat visit to my uncle Rurik and his family in Fiji, following the adventures of the Scarlet Pimpernel and Tarzan and eating the fat crimson fallen plums before the wasps got to them. At night we made charred smoky toast on a toasting fork over the fire and spread it with the jam that Mum cooked up from the golden cape gooseberries I collected on the vacant section next door, where they ran wild over the warm slab of concrete that had once supported a house.

On wet days I lay on the worn scratchy carpet square in the front room, working my way through soft white slices of bread spread with smooth butter and just the right amount of Marmite, and a pile of old *Reader's Digests*. The relentlessly detailed accounts of brave American soldiers being tortured by evil Germans and Japanese and Koreans dug a pit of horrified fascination in my stomach as I imagined myself in their helpless place. The bread and Marmite kept the sick, shameful feeling at bay.

At home I knew nothing of such horrors, any more than I did of hunger and want. Mum and Dad were not rich or even well-off, but only rarely did I pick up the slightest hint of food being hard to come by. Mum told me later that she had trouble managing on the housekeeping money Dad gave her, and often had to ask him for an advance of half a crown or five shillings to tide her over until the next month's was due. I don't know how much Dad earned, and Mum never knew either – for years it can't have been a great deal – but I don't think he 'kept her short', as women used to say.

Unlike her mother, Mum had chosen wisely: apart from being strikingly good-looking, with dark wavy hair and blue eyes, and always dressing well, Dad was the exact opposite of her father and stepfather – steady, hard-working (despite a painfully locked hip) and totally reliable. Her budgeting problems may have been partly due to the kind of food he insisted on. As far as he was concerned meat was what mattered most. I knew this because Mum would send me to the butcher's with precise instructions. Steak had to be rump. The Sunday roast had to be hogget, not mutton. Butcher's mince was not worth buying – I had to ask for a piece of topside, then ask the butcher to mince it.

I did as I was told, standing on the sawdust (I was a big girl now and no longer tried to play in it), looking up at the burly man in his bloody blue and white striped apron, never quite sure if he was really giving me what Mum wanted. On the way home I would sneak tasty bits of moist pink mince out of the brown paper bag. To hide my raids, I would carefully hold the bag by the corners and twirl it over again the way the butcher did. Once I overdid the twirl and the whole pound of mince plopped out on to the metal drain cover under the kitchen window. I couldn't explain why I'd done it, and Mum was tight-lipped with anger. Rescuing it was unthinkable because of the germs and, although she didn't say so, she could probably ill afford to buy another lot.

Going to the shops was my job, but some of our food was even closer to hand. Our flat was on the corner of Mount Eden Road and Valley Road, over a grocer's shop belonging to the Marriott's chain owned by L. D. Nathan & Co. Dad had been able to rent the flat – a huge boon in the severe post-war housing shortage – because he was working for Nathan's as a commercial artist.

On the wall above the fat boxy leatherette couch was one of his painstaking copies of well-known pictures, a cute Norman Rockwell urchin staring at the old boot snagged on the end of his fishing line. It was hinged to the wall to cover a neat square hole through which Tiny Pine, the tall thin grocer, could pass whatever Mum wanted. If anything was too big, Mr Pine would bring it around when he came to get supplies from the dark forbidden concrete storeroom in the backyard.

Now and then, though, I was sent to his shop, which smelt of bacon and cheese. I was fascinated by the big square Bycroft biscuit tin, with its picture of a boy running along holding another identical tin, with its picture of a boy running along… Sometimes Mr Pine would give me a free bag of broken biscuits. Mum would let me pick out the bigger bits, and magically transform the rest into chocolate fudge cake with a delicious, surprising mix of softness and crunch.

Besides running errands, it was my job was to set the table every night in time for tea (we never called it dinner) as soon as Dad got home from work. Mum would fold out the clever gateleg of the table Dad had made from a kitset and spread out two tablecloths, plain brightly coloured cotton covered by clear plastic with a pattern that looked like lace. On it, as well as the four sets of knives, forks and spoons, milk jug, sugar bowl and teapot stand, bread and butter plates, cups and saucers, I had to fit the brown china salt and pepper monks, the red plastic tomato, and the bottle of Worcester sauce. Then came the butter and the plump white half-loaf on its painted breadboard, along with the pots of Marmite and honey. They were there just in case, after the meat, spuds, veges and pudding, someone still felt hungry. (No one ever did.) I think my mother wanted to make sure that, once she had dished up and sat down, the only things she would have to get up for were the pudding and the final pot of tea – although Dad often made that before he did the dishes.

On the weekends we didn't go to Grandma's there was always a roast for Sunday lunch. Chicken and pork were rare treats, saved for special occasions. Mostly Mum served us hogget, or a round of chewy beef criss-crossed with wooden skewers and tied up with string. Once on our plates, the slices of warm meat had a neat curl of butter laid on top to slip down and blend lusciously with the gravy. There would be cold meat for tea that night, with potatoes, new or mashed. In summer we had tomato, cucumber and onion thinly sliced in vinegar, and shredded lettuce in Highlander condensed milk dressing (we never called it mayonnaise). We ate listening to 'Goodbye, Dolly Gray' and 'It's a Long Way to Tipperary' and 'Pack Up Your Troubles in Your Old Kit Bag and Smile, Smile, Smile' on the returned servicemen's radio request session. If there was enough meat left we had rissoles for Monday's tea.

Otherwise there was no dreary set routine for meals. The mince might turn up under crisp pastry or fork-furrowed mash, or curried yellow with sultanas. As well as dark brown rump steak, beef came in corned red slices, or shin meat stew with plump fleshy pieces of kidney. Mutton was fat-fringed chops or thick pale peppery Irish stew. Always meat came with potatoes, and a small range of thoroughly cooked vegetables – kumara, carrots, cabbage, peas (changing over the years from tinned to dried Surprise to frozen), or thick home-grown runner beans sliced into small pieces with their purple and black beans poking out. I liked the peas and beans best. The only vegetables I loathed, and didn't have to eat, were pumpkin, silverbeet and the repulsive chokos Mum persisted in bringing home from Grandma's.

Sometimes, for a change, we had pork sausages or saveloys, and in the height of summer bright pink tinned salmon drowned in malt vinegar. Mum made her own crisply battered fish and chips – the shop's cooked fish was despised as shark – but our regular Friday treat after late-night shopping was steaming hot chips eaten straight out of the newspaper.

While there was no hint of tension, conflict or Victorian sternness at our family table, and having tea was much more than a disagreeable necessity, it was not something to be lingered over. The plates were removed the minute we'd finished, and Dad often started the washing-up while I was still eating my pudding. As I grew up, this brusque getting-it-out-of-the-way business loomed unduly large. I yearned for some sense of ceremony, glimpsed in other people's houses or read about in books, where eating together meant more than just having tea, and guests were readily welcome.

I don't think Mum and Dad were in any way ashamed of their food, or their flat above the grocer's shop. They certainly had nothing to hide: the most officious child welfare officer or health inspector could have turned up at any time of the day or night without finding the smallest speck of transgression. It was more to do with their feeling that living as a family meant shutting other people out, keeping yourselves to yourselves. Tea was not something to be shared, and that was that.

Like most children, I liked pudding best. In summer we drove out to the Henderson orchards for crates of apples and apricots, plums and pears. Mum spent long hot hours bottling all this fruit in thick Agee jars so we could eat it year-round with hectic yellow custard (made with Edmonds powder) or, after the fridge arrived in 1950, with ice cream. For special occasions we had whipped cream as well. Winter brought rice pudding, or steamed pudding and fruit sponge with yet more custard – I must have eaten oceans of it.

My favourite was trifle, which combined the lot, plus scented sherry, in a cut-glass bowl showing the layers, but that was a luxury reserved for birthdays, when the beautiful tablecloth embroidered with orange marigolds came out, and for Christmas. The trifle must have appeared at teatime or maybe on New Year's Day, because no matter how hot it was on Christmas Day, lunch was always roast dinner followed by rich steamed Christmas pudding, studded with carefully distributed silver threepences and served with custard and cream.

Even at Christmas, I don't remember anyone else ever joining us. There were always just the four of us sitting down for all that food. Despite the strings of paper chains and Christmas lights, the fizzy raspberry drink and the special Christmas paper serviettes, there always seemed to be a faint sense of anti-climax and disappointment – or maybe I'd just gone flat after the day's real highlight, diving into the bulging early morning stocking at the foot of the bed.

In one sense Mum and Dad spoiled me and my sister. Both of them had had difficult, pinched childhoods and were determined their children would want for nothing that was in their power to provide, from weekly roast dinners to extravagant treats for special occasions. At Easter, Dad would give each of us a large hollow egg ringed with chocolates in a glossy white Queen Anne box. I would hoard mine in my room and make it last as long as I could, eating the egg piece by piece and moving on to one chocolate a day, carefully matching the different shapes to the chart of centres in the lid, making sure I kept my favourite green-foiled peppermint crèmes until last. It never occurred to me to share them, and anyway there was no need for such a sacrifice. Mum got her own green-and-gold double-layer box of Winning Post chocolates, and each night after tea, while we listened to *Life with Dexter* or Randy Stone's *Night Beat*, she would hand them around until they were all gone.

I was a solitary, self-absorbed child. I loved to eat and was strongly aware of food, but played almost no part in producing it. The tiny kitchen in our flat had a narrow sink-bench under the window, a gas stove, a wall of cupboards built by Dad, and in time the looming fridge, which arrived when I was five. There was barely enough room left for my petite mother, let alone anyone else. Every so often she would try to get me involved. I was happy enough to lick bowls, cut out biscuits and put jam into tart cases, but I showed little interest in learning anything more and made a mess whenever I tried. My cack-handedness reinforced my mother's repeated conviction that I had 'no brains for anything but school'.

My cooking teacher at the Normal Intermediate School in Epsom was equally unsuccessful. The curriculum had supposedly been designed for girls who, like me, didn't know one end of a potato peeler from the other. Once a week I put on an immaculate white apron, washed and ironed by Mum, and a little cap on which I'd embroidered 'Anne' in wavering red thread, and went nervously with my class to the huge sunny cookery room, where the shining electric stoves looked nothing like Mum's battered old gas one.

We worked in pairs, one measuring out the ingredients, the other following the cooking instructions. We were supposed to swap roles every week. Convinced I couldn't cook and would simply make a fool of myself, I foiled the system by talking my partners into letting me do the measuring.

There seemed to be almost no connection between the food we made and sometimes ate in class and what we had at home. Nothing was ever fried in that pristine school kitchen, and nothing came out of tins. Every second lesson seemed to involve floury, lumpy, tasteless white sauce; I carried home a procession of sad little enamel pie dishes containing awful things such as leeks lying dead under a thick blanket of it.

The best part was the baking, but we rarely got to eat any of it, let alone take it home. At lunchtime on baking days the hot grubby boys would pile out from their mysterious metalwork or woodwork classes and surround us, begging for a louise cake or a melting moment. For a few glowing minutes we would have their complete attention; as soon as the food was gone we once more ceased to exist.

At Auckland Girls' Grammar I discovered that other girls could not only swim, play hockey and drive, all skills I lacked, they could also cook. I was the odd one out. I started trying to copy them by making fudge at home. Even when it refused to set, as it usually did because I lost my nerve and took it off the heat too soon, the soft chocolate sludge was thoroughly satisfying. At my best friend Camille's state house in Waterview we would make the fudge together and carry it off to eat in her bedroom, away from her sister and four brothers.

It was my friend Cheryll's cooking that impressed me most. I met Cheryll through Debating when I was in the sixth form. She went to St Mary's College, a Catholic girls' school in Ponsonby, and lived with her mother and sister in a state house in Mount Roskill. The first time I went to her house she made pizza with scone dough, and I think she used grated Chesdale cheese. I liked this exotic food so much I took home the recipe and persuaded my mother to help me make it. The instructions for scone dough pizza are still out there on the internet, although now the suggested toppings include mozzarella, basil pesto and sun-dried tomatoes.

By then, thanks to a legacy from Uncle Frank, Grandma's one wealthy brother, we had moved from the flat to our own house. It was a 1920s bungalow in Garry Road, one of the little hidden-away, no-exit Mount Eden streets I liked so much. The house had a large, light kitchen, made even bigger when my father knocked down the wall separating it from the back-porch laundry. There was plenty of room for me to learn to cook and my mother tried again, but apart from making fudge and pizza, I was happy to leave the whole business to her.

2

Colour cookery

My husband Chris and I, with our young sons Jonathan and Patrick, are house-sitting a friend's Ponsonby cottage before we set off overseas. On her kitchen bookshelf I've found A Book of Middle Eastern Food *by Claudia Roden. I sit down and read it from beginning to end. I know nothing about Middle Eastern food, but I love the sound of its subtle flavours and colours and unusual combinations and the general lightness of it all, with nothing too heavy or fatty or solid. And it doesn't sound difficult or expensive. I want to learn how to make it.*

This is 1972, and I can't get some of the ingredients, such as saffron, sumac or rosewater, but I can get long-grain rice, olive oil and even chickpeas, although I have to cook them from scratch – they don't yet come in tins. At my first attempt I ruin a saucepan by forgetting about them until they've boiled dry. Lots of lemon juice is called for, but that's no problem – I've never had to buy a lemon in my life.

Thanks to my new feminist sensibilities I can see that this food tradition has depended on the women of the house – or at any rate the servants – being willing and able to spend long hours pounding and rolling and shaping. I avoid the dishes that will take too long, or require a machine.

I dream of boned stuffed chicken, 'a splendid party dish, similar to those featured in medieval manuals. ... it looks rather beautiful with its subdued boneless shape, served whole and sliced at table'. The idea is to 'pull the skin right off as though undressing the chicken', stuff it back into a chicken shape with mincemeat made from the cooked flesh, veal and pistachio nuts, then brown and poach the whole thing in stock and leave it to cool. I try this once but the skin manoeuvre defeats me at the outset.

But I was right, most of these dishes are easy. I invite friends around for a farewell dinner and fearlessly tackle cucumber and yoghurt salad and rice wrapped in vine leaves. (A friend has a grapevine I can raid.) I serve Persian roast chicken stuffed with apricots, and Sephardic orange cake made with ground almonds instead of flour. My friends are astonished. 'I could never make this in a million years,' Hilary says. I glow with a new confidence and pride in my ability to cook good food.

In June 1964 I had shocked my parents by getting engaged. I was just nineteen and in the second year of a Bachelor of Arts course. Although I hadn't planned on getting married I was in love with Chris, and marrying seemed to be the only way we could safely go beyond increasingly heavy petting in my bedroom or, more recklessly, his flat. In those days you had to tell Family Planning the wedding date and your fiancé's name, address and occupation before they would instruct you in the mysteries of contraception.

When I stopped and thought more soberly about it, I saw Chris as a good man who would make a good husband. He asked me and I said yes. The engagement notice appeared in the *Herald* the same day as ads for the Beatles' Auckland concert. I longed to go to it, but self-righteously told my friends I couldn't afford it as I was saving up for married life.

Cheryll threw a kitchen shower and served pizza. I was grateful: my glory box consisted of one avant-garde rough linen tablecloth and a few tea towels. But sitting on her couch, surrounded by girls I had been at school with only two years before, I felt like a child who had somehow fooled everyone into thinking she was grown-up. I still use some of the gifts I was given that night – a sturdy apple corer, the last two survivors of a set of six pottery ramekins, a flexible fish slice with the paint on its wooden handle worn away. And always on the bench by the salt box is the tall wooden pepper grinder my sister gave me, its red varnish long gone, showing the golden wood beneath.

When we married in February 1965, I was starting my third and final BA year. Chris was working as a postman as well as studying for his degree. We moved into the Parnell flat he had shared with his friend John, who had moved out because he was getting married too. In their flat John had done the cooking and Chris the cleaning. Even so, Chris probably knew more about cooking than I did. He introduced me to something simple I hadn't had before, and still love: thinly sliced, well-seasoned fresh tomato on hot buttered toast.

We never talked about who was going to buy the food and cook the meals: we both just expected that I would do it all. I had done my best to prepare for this new responsibility. Chris had introduced me to a young married student couple who were, next to John, his closest friends. Frances was a good cook – her mother, widowed early with four girls to raise, had been a home science teacher – so rather than turn to my own mother for help I asked her to teach me the basics. I wrote everything down carefully in my new *Collins Red Recipe Book*, an engagement present from Chris's Aunt Betty.

It didn't occur to me to buy myself a cookbook. I scarcely knew they existed. Apart from the slim paper booklets that came free with the fridge, the pressure cooker and the electric frypan, the *Edmonds Cookery Book* had been the only recipe book my mother owned. As a little girl I had loved to pore over its colour plates, longing for the orange jellies set in scooped-out orange skins. Mum used recipes mainly for baking – she knew almost everything else by heart – but she was always cutting out new recipes, or getting them from friends and from Aunt Daisy's and Marina's radio programmes, writing them on scraps of paper and card and keeping them in the corners of cluttered drawers, even though the narrow limits of what Dad would eat meant she almost never used them.

As soon as I was engaged she started passing on recipes she thought I'd like – Vinaigrette Dressing, Impossible Pie – and I added them to the plastic-covered pages of the photo album where, with Frances's prompting, I had started my own collection.

Frances was an excellent teacher: she didn't stick to the obvious everyday New Zealand standards, but chose recipes that would give me a range of basic techniques. Ironically, given my school experience, one of the most useful things she taught me was the correct roux method for making a white sauce, indispensable for so many dishes, from creamed mushrooms to cheese soufflé – which she also taught me to make, with stunning success. As I chopped and whipped and browned in her shabby old villa kitchen, something new, a kind of desire and pleasure to do with creating food rather than just eating it, stirred and began to grow.

A few lessons did not, of course, enable me to go straight from almost total ignorance and incompetence to being a fully fledged cook. It took me weeks to realise that our flat's aged gas oven needed at least twenty minutes to reach the set temperature and there was no point putting anything into it before then. I finally grasped this one embarrassing Saturday when I futilely tried to heat up a Pyrex dish of leftover mince in the oven for Chris's breakfast, before he went off to his work as a postie. Without saying anything, he took over and used the frying pan instead. That afternoon, faced with a trayful of ambitious Afghan biscuits stubbornly refusing to cook, I kept turning up the temperature and came back minutes later to find them charred black. Ever after they were known as Les Afghans Noirs.

My biggest problem was thinking what to have. We couldn't afford to eat the traditional meat-and-vege dinners my mother had cooked, and I didn't have the knowledge, or often the time, to make them anyway. Mostly I shopped at the local dairy, where I was thrilled to discover frozen fish fingers.

Nancy Spain rescued me: Chris's Aunt Betty gave us her glossy 1963 *Colour Cookery Book* as a wedding present. Betty knew and admired Nancy because they were both down-to-earth Newcastle lasses. She told me about Nancy's career as a journalist and her death in a plane crash in 1964, but neither of us knew that Joan Werner Laurie, the woman who died with her, had been her lover for fifteen years, nor that Joan's younger son was in fact Nancy's child. In the book Nancy refers to Joan as her partner, although not by name.

Nancy started at my level. 'I'm under the impression that there are still plenty of ordinary women around, women who (like me) are NOT experts in the kitchen,' she wrote. 'It was for them, and not for the ever-growing legion of "Experts" that I compiled this book.' She helpfully explained, for example, the difference between boiling, braising, simmering and casseroling, and almost every recipe had a picture of what the result should look like, a huge help to a struggling beginner.

From the start I was determined to invite our friends around for dinner: I didn't want the kind of closed-off existence my parents seemed to have had. Besides, 'dinner parties' were the kind of sophisticated undertaking that distinguished my new life as a student wife from my mother's.

I had been married barely a month when I asked my favourite English professor, Tom Crawford, to dinner. It all seemed simple enough. The meat would be seventeenth-century pork chops (a recipe from Frances), spread well ahead of time with a mixture of parsley, chopped onion, oil, salt and lemon juice, and then grilled. With them we would have rice (because potatoes were boring and bourgeois and I often got them wrong) and green beans (frozen, so no problems there).

Dessert would be Nancy's chocolate orange fluff, which looked foolproof: Dissolve a packet of orange jelly, beat it up with a tin of evaporated milk, pour it into a glass bowl and leave it to set, ready for decorating at the last minute with chocolate buttons, bits of orange, and whipped cream.

The glass bowl of fluff had to go on the floor because the kitchen table was laid ready for dinner in the living room and there was no space left on the minute sink-bench. Tom and Chris sat awkwardly knee to knee on the divan, eating peanuts and drinking Bakano, the only red wine we knew – there may have been others but we'd never heard of them – while behind the elegant curtain I'd made from an orange silk remnant, I worked frantically, trying to time boiling the rice and beans and grilling the chops so everything would be ready at once.

The chops weren't raw but they were rock hard. The rice was gluggy and the beans were grey. Tom bravely chewed his way through it all, keeping up a flow of urbane literary chat.

I was relying on the dessert, sitting prettily in its cut glass bowl, to rescue the evening. But not knowing the difference, I'd used sweetened condensed milk instead of plain evaporated milk, so the promised fluff had become a sickly goo. None of us could finish our helpings.

Once I knew I was pregnant we needed a new place to live. In July 1965 we moved back to the heart of Mount Eden, renting half of an old house across the road from St Barnabas Church. Mum found it for us – she and Dad had once lived in the other half – and Dad helped us fix it up, bombing it to get rid of the fleas, papering the sitting room, and laying a concrete floor in the lavatory and washhouse out the back. I enthusiastically made curtains and painted the small second bedroom yellow for the baby.

The flat had a huge kitchen. Besides a sink-bench, stove and wall of cupboards, it comfortably held a small table and chairs, and a couch where I could leave the baby until he learnt to roll over. For a while we had no fridge, but we hastily found a small second-hand one after two expensive pork chops bought on a hot Friday turned green by Saturday and had to be thrown away.

When I somehow – probably at Paul's Book Arcade – got hold of Katharine Whitehorn's classic *Cooking in a Bedsitter*, the conditions described didn't feel all that remote from mine, and I was grateful for even her most obvious bits of advice – for example, on toast: 'It sounds too simple to mention, but if you are always burning the toast and getting a sooty taste when you have scraped it, the answer is to *bang* the toast hard; and remember to wipe the cinders off the knife.'

Her readers, she assumed, knew even less than Nancy Spain's did, and her recipes were even more basic. I gratefully followed her detailed instructions for cooking spaghetti, starting with how to get those long thin sticks neatly into the pot (she managed to explain 'al dente' perfectly without ever using this fancy term), and moved happily on to Spanish omelette, stuffed cabbage leaves, and Swedish sausage casserole – although I have no idea what was Swedish about it.

What I liked best was her totally irreverent tone, and the thrillingly independent life of London 'bachelor girls' her book conjured up. These women weren't cooking for a husband and kids; they were cooking for themselves, their friends, and even their lovers. Although I didn't exactly want to be one of them (maybe I did, but it was too late for that), I couldn't help imagining what such a life would be like.

Our first son, Jonathan, arrived in December 1965, ten months after our wedding (as I carefully pointed out to family and friends) and, with great luck, two weeks after my final exams. In the new year Chris began training to be a primary teacher. He went to teachers college for the same reasons as I would go there four years later: he needed the money and couldn't think what else to do. Teachers-in-training were paid a wage and helped to complete their degrees if necessary. Chris got just enough to keep himself, a wife and a baby, pay the rent, and run an old car.

That first year I stayed at home. Thin and perpetually tired after a long and difficult birth, and experiencing what was probably post-natal depression, I existed from day to day in an uncomprehending fog. Chris gave signs of being deeply concerned, but I think he felt helpless. He didn't generally expect to be personally waited on, and he helped with housework and childcare, but, apart from some routine jobs such as taking out the rubbish and doing the dishes, he responded to my requests rather than taking initiatives. I may have felt even more miserable if he had seemed to be 'taking over' what was meant to be my job.

For the first few months I left the flat as early as I could every morning, wheeling the pram down to my mother's house in Garry Road, and staying there until it was time to go home and cook tea, or heat up the stew or mince Mum gave me; she said these were leftovers, but they appeared so often she must have made extra on purpose. Or I stopped at shops I had known all my life – Loo's greengrocer's, the bakery, the fish shop (all still there today), the butcher's and the new Four Square grocery – and lugged everything home on the pram.

A year later I was feeling much better. Jonathan was flourishing. I learnt to drive and went back to university. We moved to a nicer flat on the ground floor of a grand old house in Balmoral. It had a smaller but more up-to-date kitchen with a red Formica bench, and Jonathan had a wide hall and a huge garden to play in. When I started work the next year, our kind landlady upstairs offered to look after him.

A SuperValue supermarket had recently opened on the corner of Balmoral and Dominion Roads, so I could do a week's shopping in one go. What I cooked depended partly on cost and partly on what was available. At least a quarter of Nancy Spain's recipes were no use because they demanded ingredients such as gammon and kippers, which I knew only from English novels, or Melba sauce, which I had never heard of, but that left me plenty of cheap useful recipes, mostly from other countries and mostly for mince. They ranged from quick spaghetti bolognese made with a packet of oxtail soup – packet soup appeared reassuringly often in Nancy's ingredients – to chilli con carne ('Lena Horne's favourite') with tinned beans and home-made white-flour tortillas. I made this often, although after the first time I firmly crossed out '1 Tbsp' of chilli powder and wrote in '½ tsp'.

The disaster with Tom Crawford hadn't put me off trying to have dinner parties. Katharine's 'Cooking to Impress' section set three basic rules that served me well: get as much as you possibly can done beforehand, including setting the table – 'it will reassure people that they have come on the right day and there *will* be a meal eventually'; never have more than one thing that needs last-minute attention – 'the "complicated" casserole is child's play compared to the simple steak'; and don't serve too many bits and pieces.

I loved her breezy style of advice: 'If your guests are not to see you looking flustered over your cooking, this in practice means they had better not see you cooking at all. Heroines in novels may be "discovered" gracefully poised over a rather advanced sauce. In real life a girl is more apt to be red in the face and stirring furiously at the lumps. And remember that there is no possible polite answer to the question, "Oh, I forgot the mushrooms – would you have liked some?"'

Nancy moved in different circles. One of the high points of her career as a journalist had been an exclusive interview in 1956 with the exiled Duke and Duchess of Windsor. She managed to work this into her book, taking care to explain what 'bisque' meant: 'The Duchess of Windsor once told me that colour was all-important in presenting food. She was dead right. "Watch out," she said. "If you don't take care you may serve an entire meal pinkish mauve, from lobster bisque (soup) to sherbet…" And do make sure that the plates are hot, too. The hottest food soon goes numb on a cold plate.'

Sherbet remained a mystery – the only kind I knew came in paper bags with a liquorice straw.

Although the Duchess made no impression on me, her advice did. I remembered it almost word for word, and sniggered unkindly to myself – and worse, to Chris – when the wife of one of his friends went to great trouble to serve a large group of us an elaborate dinner of mushroom soup, chicken casserole and chocolate mousse that was entirely pinkish-brown.

As far as cooking was concerned, my closest friends and I were all floundering around at much the same level and collapsing together with sympathetic laughter over our disasters. Every new creation we attempted when trying to impress each other had vaguely foreign connections, but it took me a long time to learn how to tell a good recipe from a bad one. I subjected Sandra Coney and her husband Miles to an exotic 'Austrian' dish I'd found in a magazine: veal stew made with coffee and raisins, served with rice and small leaden dumplings – Miles struggled manfully with these before giving up. Later, Sandra served us chilli con carne. Made much more carefully than my everyday version, it had proper chunks of beef, the right kind of home-cooked beans, and real tomato sauce, but none of us could manage more than a few mouthfuls because her recipe, too, had said '1 Tbsp chilli powder'.

In 1969 my second son, Patrick, was born and I took him home to the old villa we were renting in Kingsland, the first whole house we had lived in. By now I was priding myself on feeding my family cheaply and well. I had started to understand what all 'good food', no matter where it comes from, depends on: how complementary and contrasting flavours and textures fit together, in one dish and across courses; the difference the right serving temperature makes; how it all smells and looks as well as tastes.

Much of the time, thanks to Nancy and Katharine and my own upbringing, I was using recipes based on British food. These had their own glamour, linked as they were to the country Chris came from and I had been reading about all my life.

I tackled puffy golden toad-in-the-hole; crumbed sausage-meat hedgehog with apple and onion spines; steak and kidney pie with rich brown gravy under crunchy suet pastry. Because suet was so filling and quick to use – no one had told me beef fat was bad for you, and I'm not sure I even knew that's what the crumbly stuff in the box was – I used it often with meat, and for desserts such as steamed pudding, roly-poly and spotted dick. Once I managed to turn out a perfect ball of steamed steak and kidney pudding, completely enclosed in light spongy suet dough.

I think Chris enjoyed it all, although it was hard to tell. Unlike my father, he didn't seem to feel he had any right to state what he liked or didn't like. What we ate at home was my business; his job was to eat it without complaint or criticism. His widowed, no-nonsense Yorkshire mother Marion had trained him to eat whatever was put in front of him – or on him: he told me that as a teenager he used to wake up to a plate of porridge planted firmly on his chest.

Marion was an excellent cook who had been in charge of a hospital kitchen, and Chris must have been relieved when my first inept cooking efforts improved. Marion helped by teaching me how to make perfect Yorkshire pudding, another cheap and tasty filler. We had it more often with sausage toads peering out of their holes than with roast beef, which I didn't like much anyway. Apart from the splendid monsters carved in front of the guests at wedding buffets, the only kind of beef roast I knew was the wooden-skewered, string-tied, fat-streaked, gristly roll of what was probably brisket. I had enjoyed this at home, but whenever I cooked one it turned out tough and dry. Topside came into the category of 'too dear'. I tried roasting a piece once but it was still tough and dry, so I concluded it wasn't worth the extra cost. I had never seen or even heard of a whole fillet.

Encouraged by my cookbooks and the new women's magazines, such as *Eve* and *Thursday*, that arrived along with supermarkets in 1968, I began to branch out into vaguely Chinese, Mexican and 'Continental' dishes. Not only were they cheap because they used less meat, but all-in-one meals based on pasta and rice were faster and simpler to cook than meat and separate vegetables.

Every so often I learnt how to make something genuinely foreign. We made friends with Chris's teachers college English lecturer, Augusta Ford, and her husband Bob. Related to director John Ford, Bob was a lifelong socialist and had fought in the Spanish Civil War. The couple had moved to New Zealand from California in the 1950s to escape McCarthyism. Bob did all the cooking, and Augusta dealt with the cleaning by ignoring it. They were immensely kind and generous; at their spartan book-lined house in Glendowie we stowed our sleepy children in the spare room and sat long into the night over giant T-bone steaks, steadily refilled glasses of Spanish red wine, and bottomless pots of ferociously strong coffee.

I still have the Fords' precise instructions for Mexican tamale pie (cornmeal was another good cheap filler), and a magnificent baked cheesecake that Jonathan always asked for on his birthday. From recipes such as these I was starting to learn that if instructions were authentic and clear, and I followed them carefully – buying all the right ingredients and assembling them the right way – I could produce food a cut above what even the party pages of my *Colour Cookery Book* had to offer.

In 1970 we finally managed to buy our own home, a solid roomy former state house near the Mount Roskill shops. The first thing we did was change the kitchen layout from an awkward corridor to a more practical U-shape. I loved the old terrazzo benches and wall of cupboards, and we were able to throw laughter-filled dinner parties on a handsome old table I salvaged from someone's basement.

We lived there for only two years: in 1972 we decided to go to Albania, and booked tickets to leave in January the following year. We sold our house in October and spent the last months housesitting in Ponsonby.

It was in this house that I discovered Claudia Roden. *A Book of Middle Eastern Food* had first appeared in 1968, but had really taken off after Penguin brought out the paperback edition in 1970. The book conjured up for me an entirely new kind of food and culture, but I was so ignorant that I didn't understand the close connection between what I was reading and what I would soon encounter in Albania, which had been part of the Ottoman Empire for almost five hundred years.

Another reason for my instant attraction to Middle Eastern food became clear years later, when I read an interview with Roden. Her food, she explained, had nothing to do with restaurants or chefs – in fact restaurant menus in the countries she wrote about were often very limited. The infinitely varied dishes she described in such loving detail came from real home kitchens.

Nancy Spain and Katharine Whitehorn had provided the absolute basics I needed to know, but there was much more to it than that: they were real writers who persuaded me that I could be, like them, a woman writer who cooked properly. In terms of food, Claudia Roden was on another plane altogether. She opened my eyes to a different kind of authenticity, based on intimate knowledge and love of what she was describing. For the first time, I began to understand fully what food, cooking and eating were about.

3

Revolting

My three-year-old son sits at his low table facing a pale speckled mixture of mashed vegetables. I am insisting he eats them before I give him anything else. He is not going to eat them. I don't remember exactly what happens next, although I know it's me who gives in. I can see only the stainless steel bowl of dun-coloured mush on the plastic tartan mat and the fair-haired, flushed, determined child refusing to bow to his mother's unfathomable demand that he eat something inherently revolting she has never made him eat before.

I know why we were stuck in that pointless stand-off. I'd been reading one of the confident advice columns by male doctors that littered the pages of wife-and-mother-at-home magazines in the 1960s. Children, the doctor said, should learn to eat what they were given. I must have been so uncertain of my ability to raise a child that I believed it.

I was quickly ashamed of myself for being so stupid and unkind. My mother had never insisted I eat anything. She had let me have more or less what I liked from whatever was on offer – arrowroot biscuits drowned in hot milk and sugar for breakfast, a plateful of mashed potato with Marmite for tea.

The first time I had been forced to eat something loathsome was at Pakuranga Health Camp when I was seven. I had been sent there for six weeks because I caught a lot of colds. On my first morning I was lined up with the other kids, all of us dressed in red cotton gingham, and marched into the vast dining room for breakfast. We sat on child-sized chairs at low tables for six. In the middle was a plate of crunchy-looking slices of brown and white bread, baked not toasted – I think it was what Plunket's baby book called 'scrunch'– and spread with either Marmite or peanut butter. Relieved to see something familiar-looking, I was reaching for one when the other kids hissed at me, 'That's for later.'

The staff brought around bowls of gluey grey porridge with a teaspoonful of brown sugar in the middle, and firmly told us to 'eat it all up'. Long before I'd managed to choke down most of mine, the skinniest boys were lining up for a second bowl. (I thought of them later, when I read Oliver Twist.) When I left all the lumps in a pile at the bottom, the other kids took great delight in pointing out that I had to eat them too – 'It's the rules.' When I tried, the whole disgusting mess came surging back up my throat and out on to the floor.

At eleven, I devoured *Jane Eyre*. Charlotte Brontë knew about being forced to eat institutional porridge, although hers was burnt as well as lumpy. It was the first time I read about repulsive food. Usually the food children ate in my books was like the bright party-food pictures in the *Edmonds Cookery Book*: endless happy feasts of jelly and ice cream, crumpets and cake, ginger beer and gingerbread – the girls in Enid Blyton's boarding-school books thrillingly pressed sardines into it for midnight feasts. In my mother's magazines there was no such thing as revolting food, just page after page of bright cheerful advice on how to turn everyday ingredients into 'Tasty Treats for the Whole Family'.

It's no accident that I first came across most of the things I loathe when I was miserably incarcerated at health camp, but it wasn't just because of the feelings that went with them. The slimy choko, watery pumpkin, soggy silverbeet, and gluggy porridge were all inherently nasty because of how they were cooked – just like the vegetables I had tried to make Jonathan eat, and the dry, grainy, mashed liver I dutifully prepared when he was a baby, following some earnest piece of advice I'd read. Even now I can't stand the smell of porridge cooking or the awful way it plops out of the saucepan.

Unlike many women I knew, I was lucky: my mother cared about food and could cook well, and so, after a stumbling apprenticeship, could I. For me, cooking was the most interesting part of everyday housekeeping, but it was still endless and relentless. It was the one chore you could never ignore or put off or even successfully delegate, unless you had one of those rare husbands (Bob Ford was the only one

I knew) who not only liked to cook but were willing and able to produce basic meals, instead of just showing off now and then with the fancy stuff.

I was exhausted and low that first year at home with Jonathan, and not only because of post-natal depression. I loved my husband and my son, and as well as cooking I liked sewing and decorating, but I did not love my life as a housewife. At first I tried to make friends with other young mothers living nearby, but there seemed to be nothing to talk about except children and shopping. I very quickly backed away from the various organised forms of 'fellowship' on offer: the awkward Anglican Young Wives' afternoons in the vicar's wife's drawing room, with tea and dry cake and a tactful appropriate prayer at the end; the embarrassing kindergarten mothers' evenings where we played a jolly game to see who was fastest at unpegging nappies from a clothes line with one hand. They seemed like futile attempts to convince me that wifehood, motherhood and housework added up to a satisfying life. I knew that for me they didn't.

At first it never occurred to me that things could be different, but it was the mid '60s and the first stirrings of revolt were about to surface. In my case they were prompted by Augusta Ford. In 1966 she gave me a new Penguin paperback, *The Feminine Mystique* by Betty Friedan. The distressing lack of 'fit' between how I was living and who I thought I was suddenly made sense. With her brilliant phrase 'the problem that has no name', Friedan summed up exactly how I felt. What I was up against, she explained, was something much bigger than me and my life. It was the ridiculous but entrenched idea that it was every woman's destiny – well, that of every middle-class woman anyway – to marry, have children, and stay at home for the rest of her life, except for a nice little part-time job once the children were teenagers.

'The core of the problem for women today,' Friedan wrote, 'is not sexual but a problem of identity – a shunting or evasion of growth that is perpetuated by the feminine mystique. ... as the Victorian culture did not permit women to accept or gratify their basic sexual needs, our culture does not permit women to accept or gratify their basic need to grow and fulfil their potentialities as human beings...'

This wasn't simply about tradition. Powerful forces in business and the media – and Friedan knew this, having worked in advertising – were dedicated to keeping women in the home. If this made the women discontented, so much the better: they were more likely to buy more things. That made sense. I knew that whenever I wanted a quick escape I headed for the shops.

According to Friedan, the remedy was simple. It was educated women who were suffering the most, and whose talents were being wasted at home. To resist and defeat the insidious 'feminine mystique', all these women had to do was commit themselves to serious worthwhile paid work.

Of course, we would still be responsible for everything at home too – Friedan made that perfectly clear. The right way to manage was not by getting our husbands to do more: she was highly critical of women who tried that. It was by hiring other, less well-educated women to take over the housework, cooking and childcare.

Even before I read Friedan, I was already convinced that no young woman in her right mind would actively choose to be alone all day, save for her baby, in a grotty rented flat with very little money and nothing else to do. I felt guilty about reacting so strongly to how I was living because I knew things could have been much worse. I might have 'had to get married', or been left alone and pregnant, or discovered my husband had a drinking problem. (I knew nothing about women being beaten up at home.) And I lived in familiar Mount Eden, not in a bare new house in a barren, bus-less dormitory suburb, cut off from even my mother and the shops, let alone the university.

Luckily I had an obvious escape route, a Master of Arts scholarship I'd been allowed to put off for a year. Once I surfaced from the nappies I got on with reading for the course (Dickens, Conrad, Forster, Joyce, Lawrence – at the time I failed to notice the dearth of women writers) and prepared to re-enrol. The following year my first-class honours degree won me a job as a junior lecturer.

I soon found it was not easy to combine my two lives. It wasn't a problem to do the actual work: thanks to determined women such as Sandra Coney, the university had just opened a crèche. The problem was how I felt. Whichever of the two Annes I was being, the mother or the scholar, seemed to be the wrong Anne. On one of the rare occasions when I got up the courage to go to the staff club for lunch, I tried to express what I was feeling to an eminent professor I admired. With obvious irritation, he said that of course my priority had to be my husband and children: looking after them was just my 'role' for a few years. He clearly thought complaining about this made no more sense than complaining that only women had babies.

By then I was deliberately and happily pregnant again. I took the next year off work. Junior lectureships were usually held for three years, so I thought I could return at the start of 1970, when my baby was nine months old.

'Oh no, my dear, I'm afraid not,' the head of department said when I phoned. 'Twelve men got first-class honours last year. So you see, there's no job for you.'

Reluctantly, I went to teachers college, taught in a school for a term, and went back to the college as a temporary lecturer. By then it was 1971. The women's liberation movement was about to arrive in New Zealand.

At first 'women's liberation' didn't seem to make much difference on the home front. Women, especially those with children, had a tape endlessly playing in our heads about everything that had to be done to keep our families clean, functioning and above all fed, regardless of whatever else we were doing. Even if we had a supportive, helpful husband, it was still up to us to make sure nothing essential was overlooked and to feel guilty if things went wrong.

Yet a subtle change was going on. Previously the whole business of cooking had been about women feeding other people – their husbands, children, parents, guests. What we wanted to cook and eat ourselves had never seemed to come into it. Earlier that year, I had helped found the feminist magazine *Broadsheet*. For the first time in my life it felt as if thinking, feeling, reading, writing, being a woman and belonging in a group all fitted together, each strengthening the other. We used to joke that we should be called 'Feminists for Food'. It wasn't a matter of going out to eat and drink together – not only did this cost too much, but there were few places we could go without having to brave the inevitable male leers of 'On your own, girls?' Instead we organised all-women pot-luck lunches and suppers, trying out new dishes (and sometimes showing off a bit) while we talked frankly about our lives. My specialty was tamale pie, the Mexican dish Augusta Ford had taught me.

Unsurprisingly, none of the feminists I knew fitted the ludicrous media stereotype of a 'women's libber' – a hefty, hairy, dungaree-wearing, bra-burning man-hater. There were a few vegetarians but no vegans, no one seemed to have allergies or be gluten intolerant, and I don't remember any of us openly worrying about our weight. The arrival of a chocolate cake was greeted with pleasure, and we ate it without feeling obliged to call it 'wicked', or saying how weak or bad we were for giving in to temptation.

We had grown up in an era when women were not under constant pressure to be super-thin. As a teenager I had worried about pimples and hairy legs, but never once about my weight. There was nowhere near the media exposure of skinny semi-naked female bodies there is now. I had turned twenty-two before Twiggy, 1.7 metres tall and just over 41 kilos, appeared on the cover of *Vogue,* and it had never occurred to me to go on a diet. I was gratified when breastfeeding bumped up my bra size from A to B.

Before I married I had been in the same position, in terms of food, as many married men: I had simply eaten whatever was put in front of me. The trade-off for having no choice was having no responsibility. Now it was entirely up to me to manage the housekeeping money and decide what to buy and cook. I didn't have to stick to a rigid budget – Chris and I had a joint account and he never quizzed me about what I spent – but for a long time, even after I started earning, money was tight. I was determined to be a good manager, and since the regular bills stayed much the same from year to year, this mainly meant keeping down food costs through constant calculation and control. At some level, this obscuring and suppressing of small everyday desires around food was second nature for most women then, and for many it still is.

My cooking quickly became enmeshed in a complex web of rules and judgements based on getting 'value for money', saving time, and avoiding waste. What I liked and wanted to eat did come into it, but only after all these had been taken into account.

Some things, such as pork roasts, were automatically deemed too dear for anything but special occasions, and certain luxuries – crayfish, decent steak, exotic fruit – were permanently out of reach. The problem wasn't just the cost. I wouldn't have known what to do with these unfamiliar foods anyway, and at that exalted level experimenting was unthinkable. These rules remained in place long after they had stopped being strictly necessary.

It was not as though we were in the clutches of real urban poverty. I never had to hunt through the supermarket freezer for the smallest packet of mince, wait for loaves of stale bread to be marked down, or buy food I knew was boring or bad for us just to fill our stomachs. These were still the days of cheap basic food – bread, milk, cheese, meat, fruit and vegetables – and my cooking knowledge and skills were steadily improving, along with our income. As long as I stuck to the rules I knew I could front up at the checkout without worrying about whether I would be able to pay for my trolleyload. Yet the unremitting mental weighing-up and trading-off and making-do slowly eroded my sense of what I really wanted to cook, eat, do, *be*.

4

Mish me kos

The banquet to welcome honoured foreign guests to Albania has been going on for what feels like hours. We've worked our way through salad, meaty soup, meaty pasta and stewed meat, punctuated by long speeches and toasts, with pauses for translation. It must be nearly over because at last we've reached dessert, a small dry haystack covered in syrup.

Seven-year-old Jonathan and four-year-old Patrick are going crazy with boredom. They've refused to stay with the astonishingly well-behaved children at the small side table because they can't yet speak a word of Albanian. Now they're entertaining themselves by crawling along under our white-draped table, grabbing people's ankles. Patrick suddenly surfaces and runs the length of the table, draining the wine glasses. He flops down on the floor beside the honoured Chinese expert, winds his chubby arms around the man's legs, and beams tipsily up at him. 'I love you,' he says. Then he falls asleep.

We had been sent clear instructions for the long journey to Albania. We were to stop over in Hong Kong at a hotel run by the Chinese government. (It was there that Patrick would fall in love with Chinese people: the young waiters played cowboys with him all over the lobby, hiding behind pillars and shooting with their fingers.) The next day we were to fly to Rome, catch another plane to the port of Bari, then yet another for the last leg across the Adriatic to Tirana, Albania's capital. Someone was supposed to meet us in Rome but no one did. We tried to contact the Albanian embassy but it was Sunday and there was no reply. We weren't really worried: the tickets had worked, there had been no hold-ups, and weeks ago I had posted all our arrival details to our hosts.

We had no problem getting to Bari or boarding the creaky plane to Tirana. By the time we landed in the late winter afternoon it was almost dark. We took our time, stepping gingerly down the rickety metal steps after the last Albanian had left the plane clutching his bulky parcels of Italian knitwear. We were unmistakably foreign: Chris was six foot three with red hair, and my long hair hung halfway down the back of my fashionably long tweed coat. And we were the only passengers with children.

At the foot of the steps, a large grey-serge-clad guard with a rifle slung over his shoulder held out his hand for our passports. He flicked through their blank new pages, looked hard at us, and said, 'Nyet viza, nyet Tirana.'

'Nova Zealanda!' I said. 'University! Teacher!'

He shook his head and coldly repeated himself, more

slowly this time, to make sure we understood: 'Nyet viza. Nyet Tirana.'

It had been a long time since we had left Hong Kong and we were worn out. I burst into tears. Someone must have been watching from the terminal because in a couple of minutes three men in suits came to find out what was going on. One was from the university and spoke English.

They had known we were on our way but had no idea we were coming that day. My letter had never arrived, which was why no one had met us in Rome to give us our visas. The men were clearly upset with us for taking them by surprise. The lack of a proper reception for these new Friends of Albania was embarrassing – and, we realised later, might land them in trouble with a higher authority. We were quickly shepherded through the terminal into a kind of VIP lounge with '50s vinyl suites. A '30s waitress in a black dress, frilly white apron and headband served us tea, brandy and dry yellow biscuits until a chunky black six-seater Zim arrived to carry us into Tirana in proper style.

Our move to Albania had begun with a chance meeting I had had with a New Zealand Communist dentist, Ron Taylor, at afternoon tea in Mount Roskill in July 1972.

Three months earlier Chris had told me he had for some time been thinking about how to make a major change in his and therefore our life. His unhappiness seemed to stem from the conflict between his flash new job selling glossy American textbooks and his drive to be a writer. Unbeknown to me he had been writing to Riverside, a community settlement in the Moutere Valley founded in 1941 by Christian pacifists. Now he proposed that we move there.

One short visit convinced me that while Riverside might be radical in its pacifism and its concept of community, it was deeply conservative when it came to the lives of men and women. Even so, I could probably have coped with a trial year among the apple trees. What really frightened me off was the requirement that, if we wanted to stay longer and were accepted, we would have to burn our bridges by selling our house and handing over every bit of money we had.

Ron Taylor invited us to go to Albania instead. 'They need English teachers, and I haven't found any young comrades with the right qualifications,' he told me. 'The fact you've had nothing to do with the Party isn't a problem – you two would do a great job.'

'Where's Albania?' I said, but I didn't really care where it was. What I felt was enormous relief. We didn't have to go to Riverside. We could go to Albania instead.

Today Albania merits a whole chapter in Lonely Planet's guide to the Western Balkans. Thirty-five years ago, all we knew was that it was a poor but exotic and mysterious country, a heady combination of Europe, the East and socialism. Even our best-travelled friends had barely heard of it, let alone been there. We enjoyed casually dropping news of our plans into party conversations and seeing the stunned reaction.

I thought I was ready for anything, but except for one student exchange trip to New Caledonia I had never been out of New Zealand. For the first few weeks in Tirana I was unexpectedly struck down by agoraphobia. Fear of the foreign world outside my door, compounded by my inability to speak the language, made me incapable of leaving our apartment on my own.

This soon passed. Tirana was on the face of it not so very different from Auckland, although with fewer people, no hills and a dispirited brown river instead of a wide blue harbour. There were shops, parks, suburbs, even an opera house where we saw *La Bohème* for the first time. Learning to ride a bike was a small victory – my one childhood attempt had ended in a humiliating fall – and once I had wheels it was easy to get around on my own. There were no privately owned cars, so the traffic was mostly bikes, trucks, taxis and long bendy buses.

My early explorations often centred on food. Although they lived and worked on collective farms, country people could grow small amounts of food in their own garden patches and bring them into the central market to sell. I had my first taste of fresh cherries, held out to me by a wrinkled woman sitting beside a great glistening burgundy pile. I had nothing to put them in. My string bag was already full of green-fringed baby carrots, little red peppers and the kind of lumpy, tangy tomatoes that once came from New Zealand backyards. There were no plastic bags then, and no one offered you paper ones; you would hear people pleading surreptitiously with shop assistants for 'nje cik leter', a bit of paper, as if they felt unwrapped purchases were indecent.

A gypsy woman came up behind me, tapped me on the elbow and held up a clutch of round wicker baskets like something out of a nostalgic children's picture book. I bought one, filled it with cherries, and carried them home in triumph. Along with a larger flat-bottomed one even more skilfully woven, bought from another gypsy calling out to us from the street one summer night through the high iron gates of our apartment block, that basket would later come with me to London and back to New Zealand.

That was the strange thing about Albania: because there wasn't much to buy, everyday things had great significance. Whenever you saw a queue you stopped to find out what it was for, and celebrated every time you found something new.

When bananas suddenly appeared, thanks to new trade deals with South America, most Albanians had never seen them before. On the bus I heard a woman telling her friend, 'Don't buy those yellow things. I boiled one and it was horrible.' The sharp leather-jacketed young men clustered on street corners knew better. They stood around slowly working their way down the firm columns and elegantly twirling the limp empty skins.

Rosia welcomed us into our apartment. She arrived every weekday at seven and left around two. I would make sure the supplies for lunch, the main meal, had arrived the day before, and she would cook it in the late morning while we were out at work so we could eat in the early afternoon. Although I still organised the shopping and made supper, it felt like being a married man and I did not feel in the least guilty, simply grateful.

Rosia was in her mid forties, although she looked older. Short and stocky, with small graceful hands, she dressed always in black, sometimes with a white blouse. Her wide pale creased face looked as if she had survived a difficult life and come to terms with it. When I had learnt enough Albanian to understand, she told me her story as we sat over coffee in the kitchen on my morning off.

'Did you marry Comrade Chris for love, Anna? Ah, that's good.' She had been married at fourteen to a man in his thirties, a friend of her father's, but she had been lucky – her husband was kind and considerate, and after four children, two girls and two boys, he was careful and made sure she didn't have any more.

Without the Party, she said, she would have stayed 'analfabet', illiterate, as most Albanian women had been. She was immensely grateful for what the Party had done for the 'little people' like her, and even more so for what it had done for her children. Her oldest daughter was working in a factory but was really an economist working through her 'Party stage' – every member who was not classed as a worker had to do a substantial stint in a manual job.

Rosia was well pleased with us. Not only did we have two beautiful blond boys but, forewarned by Ron, we had brought a big electric frypan and a kind of roasting pan with an element in its lid, so there was often no need for her to fire up the cranky wood stove. This was a blessing in summer, when for weeks the temperature could stay above 30 degrees.

Our incomes were high by local standards, and we paid nothing for our apartment, or for Rosia. We had privileged access to special well-stocked shops, although we rarely went to them ourselves: grey-haired Jakub, tall and gravely courteous, came around every morning to collect our shopping lists and money. In my *Collins Red Recipe Book*, brought from home, I wrote down all the words I would need, from easy – oriz (rice), domate (tomatoes) – to unguessable – patlixhanj (eggplant), portokalle (oranges).

We used the ordinary shops too, and they seemed to have plenty of most things. Olive oil, white flour and white bread were rationed, and the pretty yellow loaves of cornbread tasted disappointingly dull and dry, but the bakers' shelves never seemed to be short of the solid round loaves of chewy, dark brown, slightly sour-tasting rye bread that kept for days. We ate it for supper with olives, pickled peppers, tinned fish, salami, eggs, and three kinds of cheese: djathë i bardhë (white cheese), a salty feta; a soft curd cheese handily called gjizë; and djathë kaçkavalle, a hard dry yellow cheese like a mild parmesan, best thinly sliced or finely grated, although we made vain attempts to toast it.

Beef was the most highly valued meat and was rationed, although not for us, but there was never a shortage of pork and it was cheap. Pale and tender, from whey-fed pigs, it became our everyday meat. We ate fried chops with crunchy fried potatoes; tall terracotta pots of haricot beans in tomato sauce, studded with chunks of fat pork, smoky bacon or skinny sausages and simmered on the back of the stove; and, every so often, moist fragrant roasts covered in finely cut herbs – majdanoz (parsley), trumzë (thyme), rigon (oregano).

Rosia had no problem with cooking pork for us, but like many former Muslims she never ate it herself, saying it disagreed with her stomach. No one had openly called themselves Muslim, Catholic or any other kind of religious believer since 1967. That was the year Albania had become the only formally atheist country in the world when, following Comrade Enver Hoxha's speech at the Fifth Congress of the Party of Labour (according to official Party history), 'the people condemned the anti-national and anti-popular role of religion, religious customs and the reactionary clergy, and decided to give up religious rituals and backward customs'.

Before she started working as a state-supplied housekeeper, Rosia had been a professional cook, and her food was by far the best in our apartment building. We heard her explaining to Hurimai, the housekeeper of our Australian neighbours, that foreigners didn't like great lashings of oil and garlic. Most Albanians, judging by state banquets and the handful of restaurants we tried, seemed to believe that the more oil, garlic, meat and sugar in one meal the better.

It was hard to say exactly what 'Albanian food' consisted of. Above all, it was seasonal: beans in spring, peaches in summer, cherries in autumn, chestnuts in winter. And suddenly one autumn day gorgeous big rosy pomegranates appeared – I had thought they existed only in legends.

Food processing was still small-scale and not highly industrialised, so the jars of jam, pickled vegetables and fruit looked and tasted like the ones our mothers used to make, without any added colourings or artificial flavours. All the jars and bottles could be recycled, knocking half a lek, about five New Zealand cents, off the cost of new ones, provided I wrote 'shishe ka', 'there is a jar/bottle', against all the appropriate items on my shopping list.

At the time, I still had so little experience of foreign food that many of the dishes Rosia made were entirely new to me. Looking back, I can see they were based around variants of many now familiar staples of Greek, Turkish and Italian cooking, from dolma – with rice rolled in parcels of cabbage instead of vine leaves – to pastiço – macaroni with eggs and cheese, recipes borrowed and lent back and forth through neighbours and invaders.

Thanks to Claudia Roden I did know about dolma. I also knew about stuffed vegetables, but Rosia's were as different from those I had painstakingly made in New Zealand as their Albanian name, zarzavate te mbushura, was from prosaic English. I could manage to stuff only peppers and eggplants, the easy ones, and even then I had to cut the eggplants in half. Rosia could handle tomatoes and thin courgettes, deftly hollowing them out without breaking the skin and filling them with a mixture of rice, minced pork, garlic and herbs that scented the whole kitchen as the vegetables baked in their crushed tomato bed.

There were some dishes that seemed to be unique to Albania. One of my favourites, perhaps because it combined the familiar sweet taste of lamb with the sour richness of yoghurt, was mish me kos, also called tave elbasan for Elbasan, the city it came from. Lamb chops were simmered gently in a little water, then baked in a blanket of creamy béchamel sauce made with the meat liquid and yoghurt instead of milk, and with eggs beaten in, until the meat was very tender and the top of the dish was slightly cracked and browned. Search the internet for 'Albanian food' and you'll find homesick Albanians yearning for mish me kos.

Rosia took the greatest pride in her byrek, small crisp three-cornered parcels of golden-brown filo pastry filled with meat or cheese. Much as we loved these, we asked for them only if we were giving a proper party or coming back from a holiday, because the filo didn't come in neat packets. When they prepared byrek, Rosia and Hurimai would push back the rugs and furniture in our sitting room and spread a white sheet over the marble tiles. They would each take one end of a long thin dowel and delicately roll out the dough into one big layer, so thin you could see through it.

Still today, when I smell coffee roasting I see Rosia in the kitchen, shaking the green beans around in a shallow pan on the squat black wood-burning stove, knowing by their rich dark scent exactly when to take them off before they started to burn. She showed me how to make proper coffee. Put two small handleless cupfuls of water into a long-handled orange enamel xhezve – it sounds like jezveh – and warm slightly. Stir in two heaped teaspoons of sugar until they dissolve. (We cut this amount in half.) Add two teaspoons of finely ground coffee and stir well. Hold the xhezve close enough to the heat to make the coffee rise to the boil, then move it smartly away just in time to stop the liquid spilling over the raised edge. Do this three times, then pour the coffee into the little cups sitting ready on their saucers.

I failed to master this on the uncertain heat of the wood stove. Instead I had to use the battered round electric element, which had a frayed cord; plugged into the massive wall socket, it gave me a mild shock every time I turned it on. (So did the light switches.)

Grinding the beans finely made them stay in a thick sludge at the bottom of the cup. This was the style of coffee that Rosia, like many Albanian women, preferred. When she joined the other housekeepers for coffee, they would turn their drained cups upside down on their saucers and read the patterns of the grounds to predict the future, the way my mother used to do with tea leaves; but Rosia refused to ever do this for me.

I couldn't cope with kafé turq, the real Turkish coffee favoured by most Albanian men, where you chewed your way through mouthfuls of coarse grounds as you drank. Jill, our tall fair Australian neighbour, taught me how to ask for the right kind, kafé expres, in the city cafés. With it we ate small soft round biscuits dusted with icing sugar, similar to the crescent-shaped ones I can buy now in Wellington's

Greek delicatessens. We were often the only women in the café – women drank their coffee at home – but we never felt any hostility. Except for a few staring country visitors with ancient moustaches and lengths of white cloth wrapped round their heads, the male customers knew we were foreigners and politely ignored us.

Outside, the street-corner clusters of young men would call out, thinking Jill couldn't understand, 'You're too tall to get a husband!' She'd wait until we'd walked past before turning and calling back in perfect Albanian slang, 'Thanks, boys, I'm already married.' We'd try not to laugh too loudly at their shamefaced mutterings of apology. In summer the calls stopped as Jill sailed past the young men with her stomach bulging under the checked cotton maternity dress I made her.

Jill and Paul lived above us in the four-storey block we liked to call The Palace of the Aviators. (Pallat just means building but it sounded good.) Built by the Italians for their pilots after they invaded in 1936, its marble-floored rooms were vast by Albanian standards. Apart from a general and his family, who lived on the ground floor, all the residents came from abroad.

Ours was not the only building set aside for foreigners. Most foreigners were in Albania because they needed a refuge, and we never learnt their real names – unlike us, they used names of convenience. The Spanish were escaping from Franco's police, the Australians from the Vietnam draft. The Indonesians had been studying abroad when Suharto came to power in 1965. Although they had no way of knowing for certain, and may have felt it was better not to know the worst, their families had almost certainly been among the hundreds of thousands killed in Suharto's brutal purge.

Our social life revolved mainly around the other foreigners. We saw a lot of the Australians, dropping in on each other most days. Few of the others spoke much English, although I could talk easily to some of them in French. However, every so often it was proper to invite Rosia and her husband or our Albanian work colleagues for a visit or a party.

June Taylor made sure I knew how to be a good host. She was Ron Taylor's eldest daughter. Her mother had been the first of his two Māori wives, and after the second had died, leaving him with two children from each marriage, he had moved the whole family to Albania. They seemed to have coped well with the transplant, although they did sometimes have to explain that despite their dark skin they were not gypsies; in Albania gypsies did the most menial jobs and were openly despised as backward and dirty. An article in *Voice of the People* called gypsies a 'special problem' and lamented the fact that although stray gypsy children were, for their own good, placed in orphanages and made state wards, they would persist in running away.

June, who had married Bashkim and worked at the state radio station, explained to me that coffee was a very serious drink. Paired with lokum – Turkish delight – it was the right thing to serve to visitors on solemn occasions, such as when they came to pay their respects after a bereavement. More light-hearted celebrations such as birthdays demanded konjak for the men and liker for the women, served with biscuits and boiled lollies.

For a proper party, where everyone sat in a circle around low tables, the food should be brought out, dish after dish, for as long as possible. 'The more different dishes the better. If you can keep it coming until they start telling jokes you're doing really well,' June told me. 'If you get them to the singing stage, even better.'

Guests would always politely say no to food when it was offered, but you were to take no notice of that, nor of their protests about not wanting another drink. 'They mean it only if their hand's completely covering the top of the glass so you can't refill it.' Coffee should be served too, but only at the very last; it was a signal that the food and drink had finally come to an end and it was time for the guests to leave.

There was an even more important lesson to come, one which I think June had avoided mentioning because we were, after all, guests. Imbued as we were with the clean plate ethos, and enjoying all the fascinating new food, Chris and I unwittingly got it wrong at first. One warm evening in early spring, his students at the university invited us out for supper and dancing at an outdoor café in the hills above the city, which had just reopened after the winter. As their guests we were not permitted to pay for anything. We had got through a couple of bottles of beer each by the time the waiter brought out small white plates with two crusty brown qofta, rissoles, and a little salad of sliced tomato, onion and cucumber. By then we were really hungry, and we thoughtlessly ate it all.

We grasped what we'd done when our empty plates were removed and two more immediately appeared.

Young as they were, our boys learnt faster. Every morning they went off to school and kopesht – nursery – wearing their regulation smocks, black with a white collar and red 'Pionieri' scarf for Jonathan, white with a train and 'Patriku' embroidered on it in red for Patrick. After an astonishingly short time both were speaking fluent Albanian, and Jonathan's school friends were inviting him to their birthday parties. His grave explanation of the correct way for guests to behave put us to shame: 'Sometimes they're very poor and you just get a glass of water and one little biscuit on a plate. You only eat half of it and leave the rest, to show you've had enough.'

On Sundays, while Chris used his free time to write and Jonathan ran around the streets with his friends, the Australians and I would take Patrick to the expensive café upstairs in the huge white marble Palace of Culture, where we would sit on red vinyl banquettes by the plate-glass windows, looking down over Skanderbeg Square. We adults would order glass dishes of an Italian dessert called zuppa inglese, the closest we could come to trifle, with sponge cake and custard and a dash of liker, while Patrick had torte, a confection piled high with layers of tasteless dry sponge cake, jam, and something that looked like whipped cream or soft meringue but tasted like sweetened shaving foam. He would eventually eat most of it, but what he really enjoyed was carefully deconstructing it, layer by fragile layer.

The only other upmarket place to go in Tirana was Hotel Dajti. When we first arrived we had been lodged in the hotel until our apartment was ready. Built by the Italians in 1934, it had an elegant square dining room, with long windows opening out on to a summer courtyard, and an alluring bar offering imported cognac and whisky for those with enough leks or dollars. Ordinary Albanians never went there, and not just because of the cost: as well as being the only hotel where foreigners were permitted to stay, it was known to be frequented by the Sigurimi, the security forces.

I don't know if the general in our building had Sigurimi connections, but when Jonathan, rebelling against the constant streams of praise for Enver Hoxha, wrote in his school exercise book 'Enver Hoxha është shumë i keq' ('Enver Hoxha is very bad)' it was the general's son who saw it and the general who reported it to my boss.

I was called in to face an anxious barrage of questions. How had this happened? What could possibly have induced my son to write such a thing? I managed not to laugh, but was also shocked that it could be taken so seriously. 'He is a child,' I said. 'It is what children do.' This seemed to baffle my boss even more – obviously it was not what Albanian children did, ever.

After a disturbing half-hour I went home, shaken, to tell Chris and the Australians and ask for their advice. Next day they came with me to talk to my boss. Between us we managed to reassure him that there really was no need for alarm, Xhonsi had innocently done this all by himself and was not echoing anything he had heard from us or anyone else. After that, something chilled in the way I saw things around me. It didn't help that soon afterwards Jakub, our shopper, disappeared. Although we were told nothing official, we heard that for a long time he had been stealing small amounts from the foreigners' shopping money.

Because Albania was officially atheist, religious festivals were not openly celebrated. Christmas had been replaced by New Year, which featured splendid Chinese fireworks at midnight and Xhaxhai Vitin i Ri, Uncle New Year, who brought presents to good children. We decorated a pine branch with saved silver paper and cotton-wool snow. On December 31 a line of people came past our building carrying huge pieces of meat and great round tins of byrek or cake to the public bakehouse in time for their family gatherings. When the power cut out that evening, just as everyone was in the middle of cooking, a collective groan rose up from the darkened blocks of flats.

On New Year's Day the foreigners looked after each other. Because we had the biggest apartment, everyone came to us, each bringing a national dish. We couldn't get hold of a big enough piece of lamb to roast, and I dared not tackle cooking a pavlova in the wood stove, so we joined forces with the Australians to make roast vegetables and salads, with orange sweet potatoes standing in for kumara. The Brazilians produced half a suckling pig, cut through lengthwise so that it still looked whole, and roasted at the bakehouse until it was gorgeously greasy and golden. The Germans brought sauerkraut and sausages, the French a real chocolate cake, and we each sang songs from home and drank our way through too many bottles of the cheap local wine, trying to keep homesickness at bay.

The evening before we left for London we threw a big party for our Albanian friends. June smiled approvingly as I brought out plate after plate of savoury food: squares of rye bread with slices of cheese or salami and slivers of olives or gherkins, toasted white bread with sardines, bite-sized potato fritters with herbs, little crumbed sausage patties (in lieu of sausage rolls), and the star turn, Rosia's light, crisp cheese and spinach byrek. We started with beer and moved on to plum raki. No one put their hand over their glass.

It was getting late when they started telling jokes, with June translating. 'This guy was having trouble in the bedroom department so he went to a wise gypsy woman and got some special medicine. It worked really well. He grabbed his wife and hopped up on the bed. Boom, boom, boom! Then he ran out and caught the cow – boom, boom, boom! – and the sheep – boom, boom, boom! Then his wife heard him down in the kitchen. "What are you doing?" she called. "Po çoptoj per kanari, tha. I'm whittling it down for the canary."' But they never started singing.

5

Bon appétit

We're standing in a long queue on a clear summer night with Antonio and Beatrice, our Spanish friends from Albania, waiting for a table at Chartier, the huge eighty-year-old restaurant renowned for offering the best value in Paris. At last we're close enough to the stern maître d's desk to respond to his curt call of 'Quatre!' A middle-aged waiter wearing a long white apron and a many-pocketed black waistcoat – a rondin, I find out later – leads us briskly up the spiral staircase and through a cavernous, crowded, dark, turn-of-the-century room lined with glinting foxed mirrors and filled with the clamour of conversation, to a table for four. I feel as if I've walked into a Zola novel.

The battered bill of fare is daunting until Beatrice explains that we should stick to the three-course set menu, because it's far cheaper than à la carte. Still not knowing much about French food I play it safe, and after checking with Antonio to make sure I've got it right I ask for duck rillette, a kind of cross between terrine and pâté that I've heard of but never eaten – I've never eaten duck anything before – and it's just as delicious as I'd imagined. After it comes classic roast chicken with chips and gravy, which is tasty but not exciting, and I'm cross with myself for not being more adventurous. For dessert I eat my first ever crème caramel, because it sounds wonderful. And it is – ever since, it's been my favourite French dessert.

The waiter uses the clean sheet of white paper covering the table to scribble down our order. The minute we've finished he comes back and adds up the bill with a great flourish of his big black pencil. Antonio tells us the waiters are paid according to the number of people they serve, so they have to be quick to earn a decent wage. Even with a tip, our four dinners and carafe of house red come to a remarkably small number of francs – scarcely more, in fact, than the cost of the four knockout Colombian coffees Antonio insists on shouting us in a tiny bright lounge up three flights of stairs a few streets away. For the first time on this trip, sitting on a red sofa and looking down at the lights and the crowded streets, I feel intensely happy.

At first it was the French words for food that I loved, even when I had to invent my own explanation of what they meant. Our third-form French textbook *En Route* said that at ten o'clock every morning French schoolchildren ate pain au chocolat, bread with chocolate. I'd never had French bread, but I knew what it looked like from the illustrations. I imagined a thin dark-haired girl, who resembled Leslie Caron in *Gigi*, opening a paper bag and taking out a piece of baguette and a few squares of dark chocolate. (I always thought of it as dark like Cadbury's Energy, not pale brown like Dairy Milk.) I wasn't sure what happened next – did she eat them one at a time, in alternating bites, or did she put the chocolate into the bread and eat it like a sandwich?

I picked up other mysterious French food phrases and dropped them into my exercises. 'Pour Noël, Simone et Maurice ont acheté une boîte de marrons glacés.' I'd never eaten marrons of any kind, let alone glacés, but I had read plenty of pre-war English books where children bought hot roast chestnuts cooked on braziers in London's winter streets. There had to be a sugary kind too.

My diligence worked – my French teacher was publicly impressed. She was the only teacher I wanted to be like. Single but not old, slim, elegant, wearing smart tailored dresses under her academic gown, Miss B kept us effortlessly in order. She had studied French in Paris and spoke it with what would later prove, fortunately for me, to be an impeccable accent. She brought Charles Trenet and Edith Piaf records to class and listened with a faraway look as they sang about seeing life in pink, waiting forever, and regretting nothing.

At the end of my third-form year, my teachers recommended I drop the full art course I had insisted on taking because I wanted to be a commercial artist like my father, and do Latin instead. By then I was a year behind but they thought I could catch up over the holidays. Miss B, who also had impressive credentials in Latin, agreed to tutor me. I spent a succession of summer weekends at her light-filled Orakei flat, racing through the basics of amo, amas, amat. My parents must have paid her to do this – every so often I passed on discreet envelopes they gave me – but that was no concern of mine. At some stage she told me she was engaged to a Frenchman and would soon return to marry him. Now I knew why she listened so dreamily to those love songs.

She had beautiful embossed white china, and antique wine glasses engraved with a bee, which happened to match both of her initials. In fact the glasses had been made to commemorate the emperor Napoléon: the bee was his symbol. She gave me my first taste of what she said was authentic French food. It was ratatouille. The tomatoes and onions were all right, but I had never eaten eggplant or capsicum before and found them bitter and squishy. I hated it, but I would have died rather than let on.

Much worse was to come. Every so often Miss B would invite her parents and two sisters over for pavlova. My mother had never made a pavlova; I'd seen it only on supper tables at church dances, usually sadly squashed but still worth eating. So when Miss B told me her family were coming around on the last Sunday of my Latin lessons, I was disappointed about having to share her but knew that at least I wouldn't have to pretend to like the food.

There weren't enough seats, so I sat on the floor at the end of a divan that stood in front of a full-length window. Not knowing how to talk to all these people I didn't know, and who seemed to have little interest in talking to me, I tried to appear more at ease than I felt. I put down my empty plate, leant back nonchalantly – and crashed into a pane of glass. I wasn't outwardly hurt, but inwardly I shrivelled.

By the time my fourth-form year began I had recovered sufficiently to moon over Miss B for another year. I became bolder, hanging around the entrance to the staffroom to catch her coming out, changing my bus route so I could accidentally run into her on the way to school, and becoming, with her encouragement, an Anglo-Catholic so I could sit beside her at Old St Paul's on Sundays. She must have found all this very trying but she liked me, and dealt sensibly with me until she escaped back to France.

Some of the other girls, much more sophisticated and worldly, had noticed my devotion. One had read a book about a lesbian love triangle, and she and her friends started making up and passing around passionate fake notes supposedly written by me, my best friend Camille and Miss B.

Our English teacher captured one of the notes and carried it off to the headmistress. Next day Camille and I were summoned to the headmistress's study and grilled about our friendship and our involvement with the French teacher. Since we knew nothing about the notes, we had no idea why she questioned us with such intensity and then forbade us to sit together in class. She must have said something (we never knew what) to our parents as well, because we were no longer welcome in each other's homes.

That was in 1959. Twenty years later I found out about Pauline Parker and Juliet Hulme, the two girls who had become involved in an intense relationship at Christchurch Girls' High and in 1954, after they left school, had murdered Pauline's mother. Thanks to our precocious classmates' active imaginations, Camille and I had been unwittingly caught up in a wave of moral panic surging through girls' schools all over New Zealand at the slightest hint of an 'unnatural' relationship.

No such notion had ever crossed my mind. I still had no idea what men and women did, although I knew it had something to do with lower halves and that the crucial thing was to keep your knickers firmly on. In the upper sixth form I finally got up the courage to ask my friends. They kindly explained the mechanics, although I don't think any of them had yet tried it themselves. The most intense thing Camille and I did together was lie side by side on her bed beneath her giant poster of the Eiffel Tower, sharing a bottle of Coke and pretending we were drinking wine in Paris.

Despite having to cope with all this – and a new French teacher – I scored 96 for School Certificate French, even managing to work those marrons glacés into my exam paper. The next year I turned sixteen and was soon pretending to enjoy the bitter black Cona coffee my friends and I drank in dark basement coffee bars off Queen Street, where drippy candles sat in straw-swathed Chianti bottles and string squares stretched across black ceilings. I spent a lot of time pretending to enjoy encounters with males too, from sitting by the wall waiting to be asked to dance at church socials to enduring brief bouts of being kissed by the first man who took me out. He was in his twenties, worked at the post office, and had been introduced to me by my mother, but he had plenty of money and took me to His Majesty's to see *My Fair Lady*. He did not take me out to eat, which would have impressed me more.

In my last two years at school I became a Quiz Kid on radio station 1ZB, and earned enough money to pay for a student exchange trip to New Caledonia after I left school. One day in the countryside outside Noumea, I sat eating lunch at a long table on a shaded verandah with my hosts, a French colonial service family of seven – husband, wife, two sons and three daughters. I watched as the unsmiling father took the first mouthful of a casserole that his wife, his middle daughter Joanne – my paired 'sister' – and his Kanak servant had spent the whole hot morning preparing. All he said was, 'Trop de sel' – 'Too much salt.'

Save for a few tropical fruits, the food in the household was as close as possible to what this exiled family would have eaten in France. Breakfast was crunchy-crusted French bread, unsalted butter, jam and great bowls of milky coffee, although they made tea for me.

The main meal of the day was lunch, with at least three courses, and in the weekends four or five. First there'd be a substantial dish such as warm lentils or pasta (I had thought spaghetti came out of tins), simply dressed but full of unfamiliar and delicious flavours. This would take the edge off our hunger. Small helpings of meat or fish came next, with one cooked vegetable, then a leafy green or tasty tomato salad, followed by cheese, fruit and sometimes a little dessert – a blancmange perhaps, or a light rice pudding, although as the father wasn't interested in dessert less effort went into this course. Except on special occasions such as the midnight dinners for Christmas and New Year, the evening meal, served late when the air was cooler, was less elaborate. It centred on salads and charcuterie, eaten with the last of the day's bread.

I had no idea how expensive meat was in New Caledonia. On my first Sunday we sat down to a roast. The father, who was carving, served me first and accidentally gave me two slices. When he pointed this out, I thought he was just being kind and said, 'Oui, merci beaucoup.' He was silent for a moment, then resumed carving very carefully. When I saw that everyone else was getting just one thin slice I realised I should have given one of mine back, but by then it was too late. When Joanne later came to New Zealand and saw how casually we dealt with vast hunks of meat, she understood why I had made that particular mistake.

Everyone in the family drank red wine; the younger you were the more water was added. Last of all came sugared Nice biscuits to dip into your wine glass, like gingernuts into tea. I soon started surreptitiously helping myself to the packet in the pantry between meals. I was not even faintly hungry but they were the only really familiar thing there was to eat, and I missed the morning and afternoon teas I was used to at home. Like every other kind of processed food available in Noumea, the biscuits were expensive imports from France; I was deeply embarrassed when Joanne was charged with asking me to stop raiding them.

Despite five years of studying French I had little understanding of the traditions behind the dishes we were eating, and even less interest in learning how to make them. What I *was* interested in was sex. Sitting in the back seat of a car belonging to Joanne's gorgeous nineteen-year-old brother André and being expertly felt up by a young French sailor I had met on the beach, I felt the first strong stirrings of physical desire. Those feelings, along with my agonising crush on André, became intertwined forever with speaking French and eating French food.

I knew André was completely out of reach. Joanne had told me that, unknown to his parents, he had 'une petite amie' in the town and often managed to spend surreptitious nights with her. But he was kind to me, teasing me at the table and praising my French. At the Twelfth Night dinner, when he pulled the tiny ceramic Christ Child from the traditional Galette des Rois cake and was hailed as the king, he chose me as his queen. Although I knew he was only being kind, I was too happy to mind.

One advantage of my ignorance of French food was that I was devoid of snobbery about the food we ate at home, so it didn't occur to me to worry about what Joanne would think of it when she came back to Auckland with me. Luckily, she loved my mother's roast dinners and cold meat; to her surprise, she even liked shredded lettuce with Highlander condensed milk dressing, the infamous English 'mayonnaise sucrée' she had been taught to despise.

Since I selfishly insisted on continuing to speak French with her, she would get up early to help my mother with the housework and get some practice speaking English, the whole point of her stay.

Five years later, Joanne wrote from France. Like me, she had married young. She already had two children, Laurent and Pascal, but her life was not happy. I was too preoccupied with my own confusing life to reply. Before I married, the only future I had imagined was a vague copy of my adored teacher's: getting a degree good enough to win me an overseas scholarship, preferably in London or Paris. After that, there was a convenient blank. I had managed the good degree all right, but then everything seemed to stop and France looked totally out of reach.

I was thirty before I finally made it to Paris. It was the summer of 1975 and Chris and I were in London, teaching English to everyone from Afghans to Zaïrois at a language school on Oxford Street.

In Albania I had met Michelle, an elegant young left-wing French teacher of English visiting on a cheap Friends of Albania package tour. I kept in touch, and once we were settled in the four-storey West Hampstead semi we were house-sitting, Michelle came to stay, with her boyfriend Jean-Michel. I cooked them one of my vaguely made-up casseroles.

It tasted all right but was too watery, and she helpfully pointed out that this was because I had put courgettes in it. To my relief, she approved of the pudding – blackberries (les mûres, a new word for me) from the garden, with a well-baked yellow cakey topping.

Michelle and Jean-Michel took me back to Paris with them. They lived at Créteil, a little beyond the city, but they had a car and we drove in that first night with the lights of the city glittering all around us. We ended up somewhere full of narrow lanes lined with cheap bistros, and walked around for half an hour while they read the blackboard menus and argued knowledgeably about where to eat. By then it was half past eight and I was feeling faint. At last they settled on a satisfyingly small dark ancient-looking place, and we sat down to – what, exactly? Only one detail comes back: Michelle chiding herself for being so foolish as to order two kinds of offal, kidneys for her entrée and tête de veau, calf's head, for her plat principal – I was pleased I knew what it meant so I could avoid it.

Next morning I ate my first warm, flaky, buttery, melting pain au chocolat. So this, I thought, was what those school-girls in *En Route* had been eating all along. It wasn't. Years later, visiting a school in Normandy to talk to bored French teenagers about Katherine Mansfield, I saw them eating their traditional morning snack – a small bar of dark chocolate, sandwiched in a piece of baguette.

Chris and I went back to Paris the next summer to stay with Antonio and Beatrice, the Spanish friends we had known in Albania. They lived in a low-rent one-room-plus-bath-and-kitchen third-floor flat out in les banlieues, the high-rise, low-income suburbs that had been thrown up to cope with the post-war baby boom and the flood of France's former colonial subjects from Africa's Maghreb. They gave us their sofa-bed and slept on the floor.

While they were at work I wandered around the city with Chris, eating massive baguettes with ham on park benches – I was too scared of how much it might cost to sit down in a café – and trying fruitlessly to get him to play his part in my 'romantic weekend in Paris' scenario. When we wanted to take Antonio and Beatrice out to dinner, they led us to Chartier. The restaurant is still there, serving a thousand customers a day, but I've never been back: I don't want to risk tarnishing that bright memory, not just of the restaurant but of being briefly happy in Paris with Chris.

I revered French food not because it was good but because it was French. For a long time this got in the way of genuinely understanding and enjoying it. Elizabeth David, the first popular English authority on French food and cookery, was then at the height of her fame and influence. We were living in London when her first five books came out in a new Penguin paperback edition, neatly packed in a slipcase. I splurged on the complete set, took it home, opened *French Provincial Cooking* at the recipe for 'Tarte au Fromage' and read: 'Have ready the following mixture: a stiff béchamel made with 1 oz. butter, 2 tablespoons of flour, ¼ pint of warmed milk.'

I actually knew how to produce béchamel – it was simply the French version of white sauce, and the friend who had helped me learn to cook when I was about to get married had taught me how to make it – but she had never called it by its French name, and I panicked.

I read on for a while, through galantine, cervelles d'agneau au beurre noir, chateaubriand, sauce bearnaise, pavé aux marrons ('Shell and skin 1 lb. chestnuts as described on page 305'). Even if I could manage to decipher the instructions, which assumed a good deal of knowledge and expertise, I was completely bewildered by these impossibly esoteric recipes, which seemed to have nothing to do with the kind of food we could afford after paying our London rent, power, phone and transport. I closed the book, put it away with the others in its pretty box, and returned thankfully to Jocasta Innes' trusty *The Pauper's Cookbook*, which I had bought as soon as we arrived in London. I kept the Davids and shipped them back to New Zealand at the end of 1976, but it was twenty years before I opened any of them again.

At some point in the 1980s I acquired *Mastering the Art of French Cooking*, Julia Child's masterpiece, and began to use Volume 1, starting with the basic recipe for potage parmentier, leek and potato soup. The recipes were much more precise and thorough than David's, and the processes were broken down into a sequence of steps that made them easy to follow – although not necessarily to accomplish. (Unlike Julie Powell in the film *Julie and Julia*, I have never tried to bone a duck, and never will.)

Like Elizabeth David, Child was a captivating writer and could be just as imperious – for example, on hollandaise:

> It is extremely easy and almost foolproof to make in an electric liquidizer, and we give the recipe on page 100. But we feel it is of great importance that you learn how to make hollandaise by hand, for part of every good cook's general knowledge is a thorough familiarity with the vagaries of egg yolk under all conditions... If you are used to hand-made hollandaise, you may find the liquidizer variety lacks something in quality; this is perhaps due to complete homogenization. But as the technique is well within the capabilities of an eight-year-old child, it has much to recommend it.

As I was not used to hand-made hollandaise I laughed at all this, gratefully used my food processor, and never had any problems with splitting or curdling. I loved the sauce's unctuousness and rich yellow colour, as well as the smooth-sounding word itself, and the sense it gave me, when I made and ate it, of entering another world – one where hollandaise was nothing out of the ordinary and people routinely sat down to an entrée robed in it and followed by three more small, perfectly harmonious courses. Like crème caramel, it was one of those classic French creations I seemed to have been waiting for all my life.

My progress in coming to understand and appreciate French food, as well as learning how to cook it, was slow and erratic. Gradually I realised that, at its most basic, French food is closer to English food than to that of any other culinary tradition. The fish and the cuts of meat may vary, but the leading role they play is familiar. So are the seasonings, and the way the dishes fit together. For a Pākehā brought up in New Zealand and with almost no experience of anything beyond everyday home cooking, French cooking was by far the easiest of the great foreign food traditions to get to grips with – not the glories and excesses of haute cuisine, but the homely basics of soups and soufflés, terrines and tarts, roasts and ragoûts. The ingredients were not usually expensive – meat, butter and cream were still cheap in New Zealand – and although the recipes I chose might require a number of steps, few were complicated or difficult.

Fourteen years later I went back to Paris with my second husband, Harvey. This time I coped much better, partly because I was happier. I don't think Harvey believed I really could speak serviceable French until we got into a taxi, I gave the address and the driver unhesitatingly set off. Harvey turned to me with a delighted thumbs-up.

We stayed in a friend's spacious apartment in the elegant seventeenth arrondissement. She had a new baby and her husband was away, so Harvey and I took care of shopping for food and preparing dinner. Every morning Harvey would trot off to the baker's for our baguettes, scarcely able to speak a word of French but looking so like a local in his grey raincoat and leather cap that people kept asking him for directions. On Wednesdays and Saturdays we'd walk to Marché Berthier for a golden-brown roasted chicken stuffed with herbs and butter, or a skinned and jointed rabbit for

Harvey to cook with shallots and vermouth, along with slices of perfect brie and Roquefort that would put him into a state of bliss, longing to live there so he could do this every week.

Yet it wasn't until I was able to get properly beyond Paris, to Normandy, the Dordogne, and up to Brussels, that I at last managed to feel at ease in everyday French restaurants, and confident I could choose places and dishes I would genuinely enjoy – not just pretend to like because they were French.

In 1999 I was reading the menu in Au Bois Chenu, a small restaurant in Rouen named after the nearby wood where Joan of Arc first heard her voices in 1424. It was the only French restaurant I ever found that was both run by a woman, Eugénie Barrel, and had a woman waiting on the tables. One of the dishes offered by Madame Barrel was 'Lapin poêlé au vin d'anjou, accompagné de ses pâtes': rabbit baked in Anjou wine and accompanied not by 'pasta' but by 'its pasta', the pasta that belongs to this kind of rabbit and is the correct thing to serve with it, not simply because it's always been done that way but because it works. I grasped that the language matters because it embodies the respect for what is being cooked and eaten, as well as for knowledge and tradition.

In January 2000 I read Lisa Chaney's life of Elizabeth David (a much more satisfying book than the glib authorised biography by Artemis Cooper that came out later that year). Thanks to Chaney, I realised the set of David's books that had stood untouched on my kitchen bookshelf for so many years was the classic edition with photos by her friend Anthony Denney.

I took the books out of their box and started at the beginning of *French Provincial Cooking*:

> Good cooking is honest, sincere and simple, and by this I do not mean to imply that you will find in this, or indeed any other book, the secret of turning out first-class food in a few minutes with no trouble. Good food is always a trouble and its preparation should be regarded as a labour of love, and this book is intended for those who actually and positively enjoy the labour involved in entertaining their friends and providing families with first-class food... Even more than long hours in the kitchen, fine meals require ingenious organisation and experience which is a pleasure to acquire... All that is needed to design a perfectly good meal is a little common sense and the fundamental understanding of the composition of a meal.

This time I knew what David was talking about. At fifty-five I was no longer the tentative, insecure young woman I had been at thirty, and I was a much better cook. David's astute, acerbic writing and the fundamental good sense with which she approached French cooking immediately appealed to me, and I was sad I had missed out on these riches for so long. Not only were her books a pleasure to read, but many of her recipes now seemed perfectly straightforward. The first thing I made, and have been making ever since, was tarte au fromage.

6

On not eating

All my life I have fallen apart if I don't eat. Unless I have food soon after I get up in the morning, nausea threatens. When I was pregnant I could usually avoid morning sickness if I ate something plain and dry in bed, preferably before I even lifted my head from the pillow. I can put off lunch until two or even three in the afternoon if I have elevenses, but if I don't and miss lunch I become completely irrational. If dinner is going to be late, a snack around five is a good idea. In strange situations, my first thought is to make sure there will be food available when I need it.

In a minor crisis I eat more, nervously raiding the pantry for biscuits or baking (there usually isn't any), cheese and crackers, or plain bread and Marmite. Savoury things seem to go better with difficult circumstances. Even when Chris left us I didn't stop eating. I had to go on cooking to feed the children and I ate with them, mechanically and with no enjoyment, but eating nonetheless.

The boys took after both Chris and me. Jonathan inherited

my need for regular food: it's even more crucial for him not to miss meals than it is for me, although it took him a long time to work this out. When it came to appreciating food, at first he resembled his father: he enjoyed everything, but was not particularly interested in what he ate or how it was made. As he's grown older and travelled alone, he's come to take more notice of food and to savour its subtle distinctions.

When Patrick was very young he spent more time than Jonathan in crèches, being fed institutional meals, and for a few years he was reluctant to try anything unusual. I didn't push him, and often I would make him a separate, plainer dinner. But over time, as he saw the rest of us enjoying different kinds of food, he started to branch out – and up. If I hadn't read a reassuring article about teenage boys' enormous appetites, I would have thought there was something wrong. Patrick would come home from school, fry three eggs and six pieces of bread, and then ask, 'What's for dinner? I want as much as I can have of everything.'

After Chris moved out and Harvey moved in, he contributed enormously to the boys' (and my) gastronomic education, taking us out to dinner at the Mexican Cantina, and on special occasions to Ma Maison, a cheerful French restaurant in a basement. He had brought with him a small stock of French wine. Even at thirteen, Patrick paid attention when he drank his (small) share. As he grew older, he became steadily more interested in food and wine and cooking.

He was dyslexic and took a long time to learn to read and write. By the time he reached the fifth form he hated school, because he had been put in a class with kids who didn't care about learning and spent their time disrupting the lessons. One day I came home unexpectedly and discovered that for a couple of weeks he had been setting off at the usual time, waiting until I'd gone to work, then sneaking back home. We talked about it and he agreed to try Correspondence School, which had a special programme for cases of what they called 'school refusal'.

Although he had such difficulty reading and writing, he organised his time efficiently and worked hard. Filling in his first census form in 1986, the year after he finished school, he proudly ticked the box for 'three or more School Certificate subject passes'. Then he neatly answered the question 'What is the principal activity at your place of work?' with one word: 'Drinking'. Both he and Jonathan had worked part-time in cafés, and he had had no trouble finding his first job as a waiter in a hotel. He looked good and knew exactly how to act the part of a competent waiter, helpful but never too pushy or too casual. The people who hired him thought he was much older than he was.

He had no trouble finding girlfriends either, and they were usually a little older than he was. His success wasn't just because of his looks and stylish clothes: he talked to them and he listened. One night he brought a girl home late, and in the morning we found he had raided the wine cupboard and opened our last bottle of Collard's Rosé of Pinotage. We were furious with him, not only for taking it without asking but for not even appreciating what he was drinking – it was just easy to reach. He understood why we were so annoyed after he spent the next day fruitlessly searching the city for a replacement.

In July that year he went to Sydney to stay with his friend Katherine and find work. Although he was still only seventeen he was remarkably mature, and as he wasn't going to be driving a car or riding a motorbike I wasn't unduly worried. He had been only ten years old when Chris and I split up, and he had been very close to his father. In the years that followed I had almost seen him deciding that he wouldn't go under but would grow up instead. His form two teacher would later tell me it was like having another adult in the class.

Patrick's room was immaculately organised, and so were his clothes – a small wardrobe of good stuff, including a black linen Keith Matheson suit he had paid off from his wages. He looked so handsome wearing it onto the plane. Just as my mother had done when we set off for Albania, I stood watching him go, desperately wishing he would turn around and wave one last time. But I hadn't looked back, and neither did he.

Phone calls to Australia were expensive and Patrick still struggled with writing, so keeping in touch was difficult. He was unemployed for a while but soon managed to find his feet, moving from a pizza joint to a decent restaurant on Oxford Street, in a striking building that had once been a funeral parlour. At the end of the year his father flew him home for Christmas. 'You seem so grown-up,' I said. 'It's paying rent that does it to you, Mum.'

The next year he turned eighteen, and we went over at Easter to see him. He and Katherine were living in an extraordinarily cheap, spacious, seventh-floor apartment in Elizabeth Bay, minimally furnished with a few smart second-hand pieces. He seemed happy, and had even managed to save up the three hundred dollars I'd lent him when he was out of work. He wasn't earning much and I should have given it straight back to him as a present, but I was still feeling a little upset that he'd struck out on his own so quickly and decisively. Since he was so insistent he could manage alone, I would let him do just that. I thanked him, put the money in my bag, and we went for a late outdoor supper in the still warm Sydney evening. He ordered nachos for me, the first time I'd had them, talked about his friends, and waved to a beautiful young black woman going past. 'That's Anita,' he said, 'She's Swedish.'

It was an often awkward visit, our first with him as an independent adult. It takes time to learn how to be with your children on this different footing. Never mind, I thought, there will be other chances. I'll come over again in a few months by myself and spend more time with him. We can go to the markets and cook together, and I'll take him out more.

On our last evening we could have had dinner at his restaurant, but I didn't fancy going there, thinking it might make him, or us, feel awkward. Instead we found a small Italian place, but I think he may have been disappointed we didn't come to see him at work.

On our last morning I wanted him to come to our hotel

for breakfast. He had worked late the night before and wasn't keen, but I managed to persuade him, saying we would pay for a taxi. The big help-yourself buffet cheered him up, and he loved the giant roll-through toasting machine. Then we went with him to the taxi rank and said goodbye.

The phone call came soon after six in the morning on Thursday, October 22, 1987. Harvey went into my study to answer it. I heard him say, 'Yes, tell me. Yes, an accident' and I thought, 'Jonathan, Patrick, Mum and Dad... Please let it be Mum and Dad.' Then Harvey said, 'Thank you, Kathy' and I sat up straight and said, 'What's happened? Oh, what's happened?' Harvey came in and sat beside me. 'Patrick's dead.'

I found out what had happened from his friends; the Sydney police didn't call me, and I couldn't bring myself to try to talk directly to them. He had been promoted, and had gone to an after-work party with Kathy. She had to work in the morning so she had left the party at half past one and gone home to sleep, but he had stayed on. At half past two he had come home, and of course he had had too much to drink.

He was seeing an older woman who lived on the second floor of his building, and once before, had climbed up to her window. He knocked on her door, but understandably she didn't let him in. He went up to his flat on the seventh floor, put on his red and white basketball boots, and pushed the table in his room over to the high, sill-less, metal-framed window. He stood on the table, opened the window, which was taller than him, and leaned out, wondering if he could climb down to her. His friends told me that the police thought he must have decided he couldn't do it, then become giddy and lost his balance. There was every sign he had tried to hang on. But he fell.

For twenty-four hours I couldn't eat anything and couldn't bear the smell of food cooking. Then the cakes began coming – so many that weeks later I found one that had been overlooked, untouched and mouldy in its tin. For days I lived on bits of cake and the endless cups of tea Harvey made for the visitors. He and Jonathan fed themselves on bread and cheese and baked beans, or went out for takeaways when I was safely upstairs, escaping in sleep. In the middle of the night I would wake up, hear Jonathan moving around, and go in to sit on his bed and talk about his brother.

After a week, one kind and sensible friend left a large bacon and egg pie on the doorstep. It was exactly the kind of homely, safe food I needed to bring me back to life. It was weeks before I could face any other kind of meat, or even fish. I came close to passing out when a well-meaning friend had us around for dinner and served us whole fish with eyes.

We had no family in Wellington. Our friends took care of us, and almost all of them knew exactly what to do and not do. An efficient phalanx did the housework, saw to the music and sound for the big memorial service in St Paul's the week after he died, and organised the catering for the gathering at home after it. A strike in Sydney meant it took over a fortnight to get Patrick's body home; in a way that was welcome, because it gave us more time before the final family farewell. And from the first day a steady stream of spring flowers arrived, filling the house. They helped, and so did the weather – sunny and calm, without a breath of wind.

I didn't go back to Sydney until 1991. It pleases me to imagine Patrick had a hand in it. I'd hardly ever won any kind of raffle or lottery prize, partly because I rarely bought a ticket. But one morning three and a half years after Patrick died – soon after what would have been his twenty-second birthday – Harvey and I were walking along Manners Mall and saw a woman selling raffle tickets for NewLabour. The prize attracted me: a trip to Sydney to hear Pavarotti. We both went to the money machine for some cash. Harvey gallantly let me go first, and straight after my turn the machine ran out of money. I bought just one ticket and it won.

The night we arrived in Sydney we laid eighteen red roses on the ground where Patrick had fallen, with a card telling him how much we loved him. I hope he knew that – Jonathan says he did – but I have never felt completely sure.

We were getting *Gourmet Traveller* magazine then, and I had gone through the back issues making a list of restaurants. We went to Nikko's at The Point for the steak and incredible mash, half potato and half butter, and to the Wine Institute restaurant on the waterfront for seafood salad. (Harvey hadn't noticed who ran the place and shocked them by asking for a beer.) Best of all, we went (with some difficulty, because the taxi-driver couldn't find it) to Tetsuya's first tiny thirty-seat restaurant in unfashionable Rozelle for briny sea bass, softly seasoned oxtail in wonton wrappers, and an inspired tart of mango and gorgonzola mascarpone. It was the best dinner out we had ever had, and we thought how much Patrick would have enjoyed eating it with us.

I've never been back to Sydney since, because I know he's not there. I don't believe anyone ever gets over the death of a child. You simply learn, very slowly, in fits and starts, how to live with it rather than just existing. You feel wrong, marked out, guilty. Mothers are not supposed to lose their children. But over time you discover how many others there are like you, a sad secret society that no one wants to join and no one else fully understands.

Patrick's death changed both the future and the past: everything to do with him appeared in a different light and took on new significance. As well as losing him, I lost an unknown daughter-in-law and grandchildren. I cling to a handful of memories like talismans. Often they're to do with food – like the night he came back from staying at a friend's house when he was about twelve and asked me, genuinely wanting to know, why our food tasted so much better than other people's. It was one of my proudest moments as a cook, and a mother.

Jonathan is forty-seven now. Patrick would have been forty-four. There's an extra dimension to the people and places and even the things he knew. In my kitchen the teapot still sits on the sturdy wooden stand he made at school, its uneven pokerwork leaves surrounding the nails in each corner.

We moved from Woburn Road to Farm Road, two streets away, exactly five years after Patrick died. By then I felt able to leave the house he had lived in. On the tenth anniversary of his death, Harvey and I, with Chris and his wife Barbara, held a dinner at the Roxburgh for friends who had known him. I have no memory of what we ate but I do know what we had to drink. In 1987 Katherine had given us two bottles of superb Italian Barolo wine that Patrick had bought before he died. That night we shared them and drank to his memory. The empty bottles stood in my study for ten years until we moved again, but I have kept one label.

When my sister and brother-in-law came to Wellington for the small family cremation service, they had brought us Remember Me, a tall handsome rose with deep russet buds paling in full bloom to salmon pink. Now in its third garden, the rose is older than Patrick was when he died. We placed his ashes under a pōhutukawa tree we planted in the Botanic Gardens, on a rise with a view over the city he knew and enjoyed so much. Although the tree is now so tall it's hard to reach the lower branches, on Patrick's birthday, on the day he died and on Christmas Eve I still reach up and leave a posy wedged there. One of his roses if they're flowering, and a few forget-me-nots. Mock orange blossom, for the wedding he never had. Parsley, sage, rosemary, thyme. And a chocolate in the middle.

7

Another messy cook

I'm having lunch with my ninety-year-old birth mother in her rest-home dining room. It's Friday, which is (she's often told me) the best day to come because lunch is fish and chips. On our plates are pieces of crisply crumbed fish, still nicely moist, and limp but tasty potato wedges. Alongside the fish sit littles piles of beetroot and some tired-looking peas. The other special thing about Friday is the glass of sweetish white wine. Although hers lasts a lot longer than mine, we drink every drop.

I eat the beetroot first, as a kind of entrée, leave most of the peas, and polish off the fish and wedges. Mary eats slowly and intently, without talking, but she leaves most of her peas and beetroot and half her fish. 'Beetroot doesn't go with fish,' she tells me as I wheel her out. She's often said this before, but for the first time I realise it's not just a general observation. I suddenly remember Dad saying exactly the same thing one day when I was visiting them at home and Mum, over eighty and struggling to cope with the cooking, hopefully offered him tinned beetroot with his smoked fish.

Back in Mary's room, the nurses come to hoist her into bed for her nap. While she sleeps I go for a walk to the blank mega-mall at the bottom of the hill. I trail round the usual shops – The Warehouse, Postie Plus, The Dog's Breakfast (and it is) – and end up, as I knew I would, at the BB Café. It's hot, so instead of a flat white and a piece of cake I have an iced coffee, comforted by the lump of ice cream bobbing beneath the spirals of spray-on cream.

Mary's awake when I get back, and I feed her thin peppermint chocolate sticks and tell her stories about my life that I hope will have enough familiar hooks for her to grasp and enjoy. 'I've made the Christmas pudding,' I say. 'It's an old Edmonds recipe, the rich Christmas pudding. It's not in the new book. We're going to eat it at night, watching the Queen's message.'

'How lovely!' she says warmly, just as she did when I talked about our garden tūi feeding in the orange Chinese lantern tree, and Jonathan, now an English teacher in China, singing two Fred Astaire numbers at his school's Christmas concert. He came to see her last July. I think she remembers but I'm not sure. She was better then, he said. The staff gave them lunch together in the lounge and she talked a lot to him.

The Edmonds pudding reminds her of the Ceylon Christmas story about her mother and the mince pies. She first told me this story soon after we met and I've heard it often since, so I know what she's trying to say. At the bungalow in Ceylon, ordering Christmas dinner, her mother had asked for mince pies with the coffee. She was sitting at the long table with her husband, George, at the other end, talking to her guests and waiting for the coffee to be served, when the servant brought in a huge meat pie and put it down in front of her. 'What's this?' she said. 'I don't want this! Take it away!' 'Memsahib want mincee pie, cook make mincee pie!' But Mary can't put the memories or words together clearly any more. She can only dredge up fragments.

At 4.45 they come to get her up, sit her in her wheeled La-Z-Boy and bring her supper, a mug of thick pea soup and two curled triangles of buttered toast, two sandwiches, one with egg and one with some sort of meat paste, and a remarkably large banana. With her tray-table drawn up in front of her, she determinedly works her way through it all. Before she eats the banana, she carefully strips every long fine stringy shred from its grooves. 'The natives don't eat these,' she says.

Even though I've told her several times that my half-sister is coming to take me home for dinner, she's still very concerned that I'm not getting anything to eat. She keeps asking me anxiously about it until Ruth arrives to collect me. As a final treat I give her another peppermint stick. It's melted a bit in the warm room, and I wipe the chocolate from her fingers. The next day she tells Ruth about the lovely chocolate that lady gave her.

I knew the story by heart, but at bedtime I often asked for it again: how Mum and Dad had gone to the hospital and chosen me from all the other babies. I knew it was true because when I was five they went back to the hospital and came home with my baby sister.

For my ninth birthday they gave me *Anne of Green Gables*, L. M. Montgomery's much-loved story of a red-haired orphan, Anne Shirley, adopted by a Prince Edward Island spinster and her shy bachelor brother. I could be wrong, but I don't think they chose it on purpose. It probably just turned up as one of the 'classic' children's books (*The Water Babies, Just So Stories, Lamb's Tales from Shakespeare*) they bought me for birthdays and Christmases. I read it until its green cloth binding fell apart. I loved the descriptions of food, especially the cakes, and I sympathised with Anne when her cooking efforts went disastrously wrong.

Much later, I understood I was after something even more important than food. That other Anne's story provided me with enough clues to work out my own answer to the question I didn't consciously know I was asking: what had happened to my original parents? I decided that, like hers, they must both have died – my mother in some vague way as a result of my birth, and my father, equally vaguely, 'in the war'. It was enough to keep at bay the wordless fear that they simply hadn't wanted me.

Without knowing anything at all about the usual way of getting children, I understood that being adopted meant I was 'different'. If anything, I was proud of this. Around the time I read *Anne of Green Gables* I ignored my mother's warnings not to tell other people, and told some children at school.

They started teasing me about it, chasing me at lunchtime and calling out, 'Yah, you're *adopted*!' It was another reason for their scorn, which included wearing glasses ('Four-eyes!') or being too clever in class ('Brainbox!'). I don't think they had any idea what 'adopted' really meant – it was simply that any kind of difference had to be quickly singled out and branded as wrong. I started taking my lunchbox to a distant bushy corner of the playground where I could eat and read undisturbed.

I was about sixteen when I started to think beyond my comforting *Anne of Green Gables* story and realised that my mother had probably not died at all. Instead she had been like those whispered-about girls who had to leave school because they had broken the basic rule of keeping their pants on, and had had a baby without being married. That meant I must have been 'illegitimate'.

I was too preoccupied with boys and exams, pimples, hair and clothes (in that order) to worry much about this new idea. Far from having fantasies about my 'other' mother, I could hardly be bothered with the mother I already had. All I wanted was to be left alone, although of course with continued regular deliveries of hot meals and clean clothes. Fed up with my rudeness and disdain, my hurt angry mother would say, 'You should never have been told you were adopted.'

It wasn't until 1980, when I was living with Harvey, that I began to think about tracing my birth mother. That year, without my asking, my parents gave me the one thing I had to have in order to start searching: the adoption order showing my original surname.

Then an odd chain of coincidences took place. I saw a television documentary about a woman's search for her birth parents. When we moved house in 1981, the woman turned out to be a near neighbour and she introduced me to the people who had helped her. Another new neighbour revealed that she too was adopted, and had been searching for her birth mother for some years. I renewed contact with an old friend, who turned out to be working professionally with adopted people and birth mothers. And I read Joss Shawyer's impassioned book *Death by Adoption*.

Without all this I might never have got up the courage to start searching in earnest. By rejecting me and our marriage, Chris had shattered the new family I thought we had created, bound by both blood and love. While this drove my longing to find that other family I had never known, it also increased my fear. I needed to muster as much assurance as I could that my search was unlikely to end with another rejection. Everyone I talked to, everything I read, told me that most birth mothers – although not all – did very much want to know what had become of the children they had given up so many years ago.

For two years I was intensely engaged in, even obsessed by, the complex and difficult but totally absorbing process of tracing a possible current name and address for my birth mother. The Adult Adoption Information Act was still being debated in parliament – it would take seven years to pass –

so, while it was not technically illegal to search, I had no legal right to any information. I had to work without official assistance, and without ever revealing my true purpose to the people in charge of the records.

At times this meant telling lies. When I phoned the Department of Social Welfare I had my story ready. 'My sister's just had a baby girl,' I said. 'She's promised that if you can tell me my birth mother's first name, she'll give it to her daughter as her second name.' It wasn't very convincing, and I don't think the pleasant woman I spoke to was deceived for a moment but, as we both knew, she was allowed to give out non-identifying information and that included first names.

'I'm sorry,' she said, 'there's almost nothing on your file. But I can tell you that your mother's name was Mary, and her middle initial was R.' Because her surname was only a little less common than 'Smith', that R. turned out to be crucially important. Without it, my search may have failed.

The other vital clue came from what Mum had passed on to me over the years, a small horde of scraps that held, I'm sure, everything she knew. I had them all by heart, word for word. A few proved to be wrong and led me astray for a while, but most turned out to be right, and one led me, by a roundabout route, to my birth mother. It was about my grandmother: she had been a clever woman who wrote books.

With the help of a wide network of well-placed women friends, long hours in the archives and some good luck, I pieced these scraps together. During the Second World

War, the *Bay of Plenty Times* had printed fund-raising collections of poetry by a woman with the right surname. Before the war she had been the only woman of that name at her address in the electoral roll, but her wartime entry was followed by one for a second woman of the same surname and the first names Mary R. It seemed likely that this was her daughter.

By the early 1950s Mary R. had disappeared from the roll. I spent weeks putting in requests for a bride with her name for all the possible intervening years, and at last I found her. She had married a man with a much more uncommon surname, and they were still living in the same electorate.

The first time we met, she gave me some of her home-made fudge cake. It was just like Mum's, only Mary put ginger in hers. By then we'd been writing to each other for three years. Once I had sent the first carefully worded letter and she had nervously replied, I felt I should leave every further move up to her to make when and if she wanted. So all I had done was send a photo and ask for one in return.

At Easter it arrived with a card. 'Thank you for the photo you sent at Christmas. I shall treasure it... The enclosed is the best I can send, it was taken last November. Thank you for the details on the back of your photo. They mean a lot to me. I will be in touch from time to time. Mary.'

The doctor who arranged my adoption must have felt pleased with the match he'd made. Mary, like Mum, was a short pretty woman who had once had wavy brown hair –

although at eighty Mum was still colouring hers, while Mary's was greying in the pepper-and-salt way mine is now. Above all, Mary looked very much like me.

I didn't believe she would stay content with letters and I was right, although it took her a long time to take the next step. One day the phone rang, and a precise English voice I had never heard before said, 'This is Mary. We're coming down to visit friends in Kāpiti next week. Would you like to meet?'

Three months later I sat down to dinner in Mary's house for the first time. Despite being forty-one I felt like a nervous child, leaping up to help in the kitchen, scared of doing or saying something wrong, feeling I had to be on my very best behaviour. Even so, I managed to enjoy Mary's tender home-killed baked chicken with stuffed tomatoes, her luscious home-preserved brandied fruit, and the fudge cake we had with our cup of tea. Like Mum, Mary was a good cook, but she also had the advantage of a large garden and orchard, hens and eggs, farm meat, and fresh fish caught by her lovely husband. He had always known about me, and from the first day he treated me with unfailing warmth and kindness.

Like Mum and me, Mary had grown rounder with the years: we all took great pleasure in food. Like her own formidable mother, who had died two years before I reappeared, but completely unlike Mum, she was keen on joining and often leading groups of women who enjoyed getting together for some good purpose, so she did a great deal of baking, and it was the kind of cooking she liked most. The well-worn tins in her pantry were never empty.

Like Mum, she loved going out for coffee, lunch or dinner. In Wellington we discovered her astonishing capacity for eating curry. We would take her out with friends of ours who enjoyed her company, and with whom she got on really well, set a good range of dishes in front of her – from her favourite butter chicken to a pretty hot vindaloo – and delight in seeing her happily work her way through them all.

Mary had been born in 1920 on a tea plantation in what was then Ceylon. She had seen her father eating string hoppers every morning for breakfast, fed buns to elephants from her nursery window, and watched the servants using saucers of milk to lure cobras out from behind the cushions on the verandah chairs. She had been sent to a small boarding school in England at the age of ten, and had seen her mother only once in the next six years. I used to think that colonial children were sent back to England to save them from sickness. From what she told me, it seems to have been mainly to make sure they were not spoilt by indulgent amahs and the warm spicy pleasures of the East, but would instead acquire a proper English indifference to their own comfort, and especially to food. 'Once you've been to boarding school,' Mary said, 'you can eat anything.'

Her parents had retired to New Zealand when she was sixteen, and she had sailed out to join them with a trunk full of new evening dresses, and plenty of young men as dance partners. They soon sent her off again for a final year at a boarding school in Hamilton, but at least she could come home for the holidays. There was one other new girl, Gypsy, in her class, and the pair became lifelong friends.

In the main street of Mary's hometown I found an Indian café that did a special lunch deal of curry with naan and rice. When I took Mary there and daringly suggested we have a light beer, she perked up, just as Mum would do when Harvey offered her a whisky. Later she told me she had gone to the café again for a birthday lunch with Gypsy. 'I asked her if she thought it would be all right to share one of those light beers – there's so little alcohol in it – but she didn't think that was a good idea,' she said. I could hear the disappointment in her voice.

When Mary went into the rest home she could still walk, and every day she would push her walker slowly down the hall to share a Bible reading with her friend. It was only after Gypsy died that Mary's mind began to show signs of confusion and decline. Then she fell and broke her hip and didn't walk again. She died six months after her ninety-second birthday. My sisters and I all wore something blue, her favourite colour, to her flowery funeral.

Mum had died ten years earlier, at ninety-five. I never told her about Mary. I thought then, and still think, that knowing I was seeing my birth mother would have been too painful for her to cope with.

For the first few years, every time Mary and I met, I was constantly watching out for reassuring clues about where my own quirks of character and behaviour came from, so when she came to stay and I put together a nice little vase of flowers for the table and she said with a certain relish, 'Very clever – you get that from your mother', I was filled with pleasure.

But what gave me even more joy was the time she asked me, 'Are you a messy cook?'

'I'm an *extremely* messy cook.'

With a note of satisfaction, she said, 'So am I.'

It's true that as a cook, I am much more like Mary than my neat, tidy, precise little Mum, who couldn't bear the mess whenever I tried to make anything in her kitchen. But it's the taste of Mum's food I remember best and her recipes I use now. Except for fudge cake.

8

Dinner for two

*I'm at the Romney Arms, where you choose your own steak,
having an editorial lunch with Harvey McQueen. We were
introduced five weeks ago by my new boss, Rosemary, who
runs educational publisher Longman Paul. Her firm bought
Reed Education, where I was editor, and she acquired me as
part of the deal.*

*Harvey is doing an important school poetry anthology,
but it's slow going – he's very busy. Before Rosemary took
me to meet him in his office at the Education Department,
she said, 'Be tactful but encourage him to get on with it.'
The next day Chris sent a telegram to my new office in Book
House telling me he'd left me. After that I was off work for
a week. As soon as I got back, Harvey phoned. 'I've done
some more – shall I bring it over? Would you like lunch?' I
didn't need to encourage him.*

*He came again the next week, and the next, and of course
I told him about Chris, and he listened and was warm and
kind. Now we're facing each other across the table, waiting*

for our steaks. My hand is resting on the red cloth. He gently moves his closer until our little fingers are touching and says, 'I'd like to get to know you better.'

The first night Harvey came to my house for dinner I made him my Albanian specialty, lamb baked in yoghurt, but even that didn't put him off. Two months later he had left his wife and was living in a flat on his own: we both needed a breathing space to see if the relationship would work. One night he invited me round for dinner – his version of chicken marengo, with olives, mandarins and red wine. I was enormously impressed. No man had ever cooked me a dinner from scratch before.

When he came to live with me and the boys at the beginning of 1980, I soon found out this was the one dinner dish, other than basic chops, mince or sausages, that he knew how to cook. However, he could also make cheese toasties, scrambled eggs, a good beer-based Welsh rarebit, and the kids' favourite, pancakes. Like my mother, Harvey mixed the batter by eye and instinct, rather than measuring exact amounts of flour and milk, and it was impeccable: after he'd made thick pancakes for himself and the boys I could use it to make the beautiful thin crêpes I preferred. He never varied what he put on his pancakes – lemon juice and white sugar. Once he found something he really liked, he stuck with it.

Soon after he moved in, he told me he wanted to do more cooking. In *This Piece of Earth,* the memoir he wrote many years later, he said he saw cooking as creative, like gardening, a change from 'the projects and papers and reports cluttering up my existence' and 'an opportunity to do things my way'.

Harvey's expanded interest in cooking changed my life. Once he started taking regular turns in the kitchen it was no longer solely up to me to do the thinking, shopping and cooking required to put a good dinner – any dinner – on the table every night. Having someone else share the responsibility renewed my rather jaded interest and pleasure in cooking.

As Harvey's skill and confidence grew, he branched out. He loved being able to put a successful dish on the table, especially if he'd partly invented it. I used to tell him I must be the only woman in Wellington coming home from work to, say, venison with sour cherries, in a sauce made with cream, Dijon mustard and the cook's own home-made crab-apple jelly.

Of course it took him a long time to get to this stage, and in the process I discovered I knew much more about cooking than I thought I did. Although Harvey was eager to learn, at first he didn't grasp how much there was to take in – all the small but vital ways of doing things that make the difference between failure and success, or between food that's passable and food that's memorably good.

Being creative and doing it his way was all very well, but he soon realised there were some rules that couldn't be broken, usually after he'd done just that. Never mix any kind of thickening with hot liquid, because it will go lumpy. Separate eggs into two bowls before you start cooking. Reduce wine for a casserole over a high heat before adding (or putting back) the other ingredients. Always rest roasted or fried meat before eating it. Even casseroles benefit from a rest, which is partly why they often taste even better the next day.

Harvey soon became our casserole expert. At the beginning he had been inclined to put in too many different flavours, but he worked out it was better to have just a few compatible herbs than the whole garden. He also learnt not to use too much liquid; at first he had been convinced casseroles would dry out in the oven, so the juices, while delicious, had been too copious and thin. He loved potatoes and learnt how to make a very good mash, and he introduced boiling cloves of garlic with the pieces of potato, then mashing it all together with lots of butter and very little milk.

As much as I welcomed his increasing involvement in the kitchen, my reaction was oddly ambivalent. Although I enjoyed and praised his cooking, I would also mention, just in passing, that it could have done with a little more or less time in the oven, a little less liquid, a fraction less salt… I think I was intent on maintaining my position as the expert. Harvey was very tolerant, although sometimes justifiably irritated.

Perhaps there wasn't all that much of a gap between my behaviour and that of the patriarchal Frenchman in New Caledonia proclaiming, 'Too much salt.' Yet there was one important difference – I regularly cooked too, whereas that man never did. And I never criticised Harvey's cooking in front of invited friends, any more than he did mine. We knew men (it was always men) who did this to their wives and we hated it. Every so often, though, he did embarrass me by well-meant but misplaced praise – like the time he announced proudly to a well-to-do guest who had arrived at short notice, 'Anne made this soup from the outside leaves of lettuce!' Even though potage du père tranquille was a good French recipe, I cringed at having my economy exposed.

For eight years Harvey kept a daily journal; he would later use it as a source for *This Piece of Earth*, which was centred on his garden in Farm Road. Most days he noted what he or we ate, and often commented on his own cooking, although he was tactfully reticent about my failures. Reading the journal has brought back to me much I thought I had forgotten, all those apparently ordinary days that added up to our life together.

Gardening was always Harvey's first love but cooking came a close second. And he believed in pulling his weight around the house, as his stepfather had done. But when he shopped or cooked or washed the dishes, he didn't have to deal with the sense of obligation I felt, and sometimes resented, when I did these things: they were part of what 'woman/wife/mother' meant in a way they were not for a man.

I don't think he ever quite understood the depth of this difference between us, although he was aware he felt similarly about other things, including keeping the garden up to scratch – that was what men were supposed to do. In *This Piece of Earth*, he told a story from our first year together that perfectly embodied our presumed roles three decades ago:

> One weekend Anne was at a conference so I prepared the meal. I forget what meat I cooked but the dessert I remember. When I went to work on the Monday a colleague asked, had I done anything exciting over the weekend? I said, 'I made a lemon meringue pie.' 'Why?' he asked. 'Can't Anne cook?'

Tackling a lemon meringue pie at such an early stage in his cooking career was typical of Harvey. Like Julia Child, he was fearless in the kitchen, much more so than I was. This was partly because he didn't labour under any imposed expectation that he ought to be a good cook – his being able to cook anything at all was seen by most people as remarkable – but it was also part of his character to make sudden daring leaps into unknown territory, as he'd done when he came to live with me.

At Farm Road I acquired a gorgeous new recipe book, Judith Olney's *The Joy of Chocolate*. I'd bought it to give someone as a present but hadn't been able to part with it. It was full of the irreverence I liked. 'When working with chocolate,' Olney wrote, 'always wear brown.' And 'Always serve too much hot fudge sauce – it makes people overjoyed and puts them in your debt.' I was in awe of its astonishing photos of improbable chocolate creations such as the perfectly detailed cabbage, each leaf moulded on the real thing.

I knew I'd never try to make these things and sorted out the manageable ones instead. For Harvey's birthday, I came up with an inspired pairing of two relatively simple recipes that looked deceptively light but were really deliciously rich: elegant beige chocolate meringues using six egg whites, and an equally elegant whisky-flavoured chocolate mousse using six yolks. (I knew anything flavoured with whisky would appeal to Harvey.) I christened all this Le Cochon Entier – The Whole Hog.

For my next birthday Harvey wanted to surprise me too, so he embarked on Pink Pears on a Chocolate Tart. This formidable recipe was supposed to be 'made and composed shortly before eating'. It required him to poach fresh pear halves in raspberry syrup, then combine ground nuts, beaten egg whites and sugar, spread the mixture on baking paper to form a large round base with a small rim at the edge, bake it, transfer it intact to a serving plate, and give it a smooth coating of melted chocolate. The next step was to place the pears on top, brush them with redcurrant jelly, and 'drizzle the remaining chocolate over the tops of the pears in a light, lacy pattern'.

Unfortunately he didn't know (and hadn't read the instructions at the front of the book) about the right kind of couverture chocolate and how to melt it properly, so his attempt to spread a smooth coating of dark chocolate over the base, never mind drizzle it over the poached pink pears, was doomed. To his distress he ended up with rough little gobs of chocolate stuck randomly all over the top. He sensibly ignored the final decoration, mint leaves and crystallised rose flowers to be 'sprinkled in five or six spots about the tart'.

I was amazed he'd taken on this challenge – despite my superior knowledge and experience, I wouldn't have dared. The combination of crunchy meringue, soft pear, sharp redcurrant and rich chocolate was sublime.

Harvey had an enduring fondness for bright red saveloys, a childhood treat, and powdered Maggi mushroom soup, just as I do for bought gingernuts and soft white bread, but beyond the grocer's shelves his childhood food sources had been much better and more varied than mine. I envied his growing up on farms around Little River on Banks Peninsula, where the cooking was basic but the quality of the ingredients was second to none – home-killed mutton, beef, pork, locally caught rabbit, flounder, whitebait, crayfish, home-grown fruit and vegetables, and even for a time home-made butter and bread. He had formed his excellent palate on these fresh natural foods, raised, caught and cooked by his family and their neighbours. With his garden, he gave me back what my own parents had managed to grow in their tiny backyard: crisp lettuce and runner beans, tiny new potatoes, bunches of sweet peas. And he brought me entirely new pleasures: rocket and land cress, freshly dug yams – which he baked in orange juice and marsala – and blackcurrants from his own bushes.

He preferred some of his vegetables raw, a legacy of his old habit of eating them small and sweet, straight from the plant or the earth. At lunchtime he would happily crunch into big chunks of raw onion, pepper, carrot, celery and cucumber. He loved some of the more unusual parts of animals too, such as pigs' trotters and tinned lambs' tongues. Whenever he went down to see his mother Betty in Christchurch, she would make pork brawn from scratch for him. Once she got a bit behind and we arrived to find her taking the tomahawk to a whole pig's head on the newspapered kitchen floor. I could cope with her peppery, neatly pressed brawn, but not with tongues or trotters, and eventually I got up the courage to tell Harvey I really didn't care for his beloved pickled pork either. After that he cooked it when I was away, along with the silverbeet and roast pumpkin I never served.

In his absence I would cook myself liver, which Harvey hated, or a meatless dinner such as potato curry or eggplant parmigiana. Eggplant was one of the few vegetables he detested in any form.

We sometimes had two different dinners. Whenever I saw good fresh flounder for sale, I'd bring one home for Harvey to delicately dissect, while I had some other (to my taste less bony, muddy) fish. On his blog, he recalled how flounder carried him back to boyhood:

Uncle Charley [his mother's brother] and Uncle Tom [who married his mother's sister] had a boatshed and a dinghy at Jones Bay in Akaroa Harbour, a small rocky inlet between Barry's Bay and French Farm. When the tide was right the extended family would drive over to scramble down a steep clay track through mānuka, buddleia and broom, to picnic on the beach and go floundering… While the men rowed out it was my task to sit in the stern and play out the net with its sinkers and floats… Mid afternoon the net was pulled in, all hands to the task, with a few cod, the odd puffer fish, lots of crabs and usually a good feed of flounder for every household. That evening, Mum deftly handling two large frying pans on the wood stove, we would feast in relays on the succulent fresh fish.

He adored whitebait even more, and always cooked them for his birthday on September 13, just after the season opened, with the absolute minimum of egg to bind the tiny fish into patties. While I liked them well enough I wasn't nearly as keen as him and would have scallops instead, seared briefly in butter and sauced with vermouth and lemon.

He loved bringing in his own home-grown harvest, even if it was only a few fresh courgettes destined for thinly sliced raw courgette salad, a recipe he found in Claudia Roden's *The Food of Italy*. He brought home new food books, too, and soon discovered the collected works of M.F.K. Fisher; he kept the book by his bed and for years would reread a piece every night, relishing Fisher's evocative, intimate, apparently effortless writing. One of his best finds was *The Lazy Cook,* useful for a novice because it simply gives a method, such as flash-roasting or pan-grilling, then explains how to use it for different ingredients and with various marinades. He was pleased when I brought home from a Kirkcaldie and Stains' sale exactly the right kind of ridged frying pan for pan-grilling, one of the simplest and best ways to deal with good steaks and chops.

Roasts were Harvey's all-time favourite dinners, and soon became his domain. For a few years he tended to leave them in the oven too long, until we realised the culprit was an old-fashioned meat thermometer showing 'done' temperatures that were too high. Even then, it took me a while to persuade him to leave lamb and beef rosy, and to agree that pork and chicken could be safely cooked just long enough to kill off anything nasty lurking in them, while remaining moist and juicy.

It mattered because for years we had a giant roast of pork every Christmas, and Harvey, helped by one of our male friends, always took charge of the entire main course – except for the legendary Christmas of 1990, when David Lange, his former boss, and Margaret Pope were coming. The day before, Harvey was washing the concrete front steps when he slid down them backwards on a sheet of water. He could have broken his back, and for a long dreadful moment I thought he had, until he lifted his head and told me to bring the brandy. He'd cracked his ribs and had to spend the whole holiday sitting down, while I raced round trying to fill the very large gap. Only in the last few years have I begun to feel I can manage a roast as well as he could.

He was instinctively a meat or fish and potatoes man, with plenty of vegetables, fruit and herbs thrown in. Even his soups usually featured flesh of some kind. (Pea and ham was fine when not too salty, but one day I drew the line at eating any more mutton broth.) Although he loved cheese, butter, and cream – always runny for him and whipped for me – I was much keener than he was on meals based around eggs and dairy foods, and on rice and pasta.

I also had a much sweeter tooth than he did, the legacy of my school holidays at home with Mum, when we'd end a shopping trip to town by stopping at the Mount Eden Cake Shoppe for delicate butterfly cakes, cream-filled lamingtons, thick custard squares, or fruit squares, known to us as fly cemeteries.

If I made a cake for visitors I knew I would end up eating most of it. I always knew exactly how much was left and could see it sitting in the tin and hear it calling to me when I made a cup of tea, while he wouldn't even remember it was there. The only time he ever growled at me about my eating was when he'd made his usual Easter treat of pashka – a lethally rich dessert of cream cheese and butter mixed with vodka-soaked dried fruit that the boys teasingly called 'cholesterol city' – and there was a sizeable lump left in the fridge. He came looking for it after dinner the next night and it was gone. 'Did you eat it all?' he said and, when I confessed, 'You greedy pig!'

His eyes, unlike mine, were never too big for his stomach. He ate exactly what he wanted and as much as he wanted, no more and no less. The poet Jan Kemp, who had been in Harvey's class when he had started teaching at Morrinsville College in 1962, wrote a piece for his memorial service calling him 'slender as an ironing board', and for most of our life together he stayed much the same size.

By the time we moved to Farm Road in 1992, we were cooking dinner week and week about, a good arrangement:

one person did the shopping, planned the week's meals, and dealt with the leftovers. (I should have done all the dishes when it was his week, as he did when it was mine, but I was a bit lazy – I hate washing up – and he often did more than his fair share.)

Over the years this plan varied, depending on what else was going on. When Harvey worked full-time in stressful jobs, I did more during the week and he took over at weekends, but after he finally retired from education work and I was doing a doctorate, we swapped around. Later he wrote in his blog: 'Anne and I had been happy in that house… But it was more than happiness. We shared command in the garden, kitchen and house.'

When Harvey was cooking, he would often go out to buy whatever he fancied in the way of fresh meat and fish. When I was cooking, I would begin by looking at what was already in the freezer or fridge and put my experience to work making cheap meals with rice or pasta, or using up leftovers in ways that wouldn't have occurred to him. He must have sometimes wondered why I often cooked differently from him. It shows in his journal, where he simply states: 'Anne made a quiche'; or 'Anne made pasta sauce from the leftover casserole'.

What really impressed him was the afterlife of the two ducks that eventually replaced the Christmas pork, in order to suit fewer people with smaller appetites. Nothing was wasted. The duck scraps, stuffing and gravy, mixed with chicken livers, became a bacon-wrapped terrine for Boxing Day. I kept the ducks' fat for frying lacy brown potatoes, and turned their carcasses into stock, which I used to make an Elizabeth David recipe for an unusual mushroom soup thickened with breadcrumbs.

Overall, we learnt from each other. He taught me not to count the cost unduly or cut too many corners, to go for the good stuff and eschew the inferior, to enjoy the pleasures of food more, including the odd dinner out, without worrying. And of course, thanks to him, we had a considerably better income than I'd been used to, so that helped. I taught him how to shop sensibly for staples, look for specials, spot the best buys that week and plan ahead. And I taught him the pleasures of making love before dinner, rather than after.

From the start we often did the weekend shopping together, a new and happily companionable experience for me, although I had to be the one pushing the trolley or I couldn't think straight. He became a good, confident shopper on his own too, sometimes taking Patrick or Jonathan and coming home triumphant with a bargain they'd picked up.

Eating dinner – with the boys until they each left home, then just the two of us – was a kind of symbol of our life together. Almost every night it was an occasion – no candles, Harvey feared them, but a well-laid table, more than one course, often music, usually wine, and always conversation. Harvey kept a good modest cellar, pulling out interesting bottles when we entertained friends; mostly on such occasions he would do the main course.

His energy and enthusiasm for cooking got a noticeable boost after he finally retired (for the third time) in mid

2002. He had been a highly effective and energetic educator, manager and political aide but, unlike many men I knew, he had a genius for retirement, based on his profound enjoyment of everyday pursuits and pleasures.

We had friends around for dinner more often. In his journal he recalled the four who came on the last day of August that year:

> I cooked a leg of lamb with the red pepper crust...The meal was real NZeal. A lettuce salad with bread which included nine different leaves from my garden. The lamb was as usual delicious and I cooked the kumara mash to go with it and as often happens second time round it was better – one learns to mix and match ingredients. Anne had cooked a white onion confit which complemented it very well while the gravy with all the pepper and garlic was divine. Anne then produced her prunes cooked in port with chocolate and tamarillo sauce and home-made meringues. Lovely wines to complement it, Goldwater Dog Point Sauvignon, Mills Reef Merlot Cabernet. Jock brought wine from the Rhône region and Joanna a Morton Estate The Mercure, which was superb. It is one of the best meals we have made. People were at ease with one another, it was a good evening.

9

Too much

To celebrate our twentieth wedding anniversary we've come right up north, where I've never been, to an apartment for two ('not suitable for children') between Cable Bay and Coopers Beach, with a terrace perched over the cliffside garden looking out to sea. For our anniversary dinner we go to The Slung Anchor in Mangōnui, and I take home their recipe for the creamy lemon dessert the menu calls 'prosset'. But what we enjoy most is collecting whatever local food and wine we can find on our explorations up the east and west coasts – lumpy purple potatoes, tiny local grapes, our first viognier. I put it all together in the plastic-screened kitchen, and we savour it slowly on the terrace at sunset.

I can't help noticing how long it takes Harvey to climb the steep path to the ancient pōhutukawa trees on the hilltop at Butler Point, and how he no longer wants to walk the length of each lovely beach; it used to be me who said it was too far.

We had always said we would leave Farm Road when Harvey's beloved garden became too much for him. After we got back from our holiday he had three falls, which he put down to being careless or clumsy. By the time my PhD was conferred in May 2006, he was finding it increasingly difficult to cope with our three-level section.

In September he turned seventy-two, and soon after his birthday I tentatively suggested we think about moving. I was surprised when he instantly agreed. Months later, when we were packing up, he told me he'd already thought we should move but hadn't liked to suggest it because he thought I'd be upset.

Moving wasn't an entirely pragmatic decision – we'd been in Farm Road for fifteen years, the longest we'd lived anywhere, and we both felt like a change. Most of our friends thought we were mad. They loved our historic house and our garden and our dinners, and they hadn't noticed Harvey's diminishing strength and stamina, which didn't seem to improve despite his regular sessions at the gym.

I realised I did not want to do up another old place. After weeks of looking, I found a sunny, spacious, modern townhouse in the nearby suburb of Karori, a minute on foot from the bus and ten from the supermarket, with a wall of built-in bookshelves and plenty of room for visitors. Harvey looked forward to walking down to the library and up to the butcher and growing raised pots of herbs and lettuce in the flat L-shaped garden, surrounded by the neighbours' fine trees and with plenty of birds for him to watch and feed.

We bought it in December. By the time we moved in April Harvey could hardly make it up even the smallest slope, although he could manage stairs if he used the rail and took them slowly. The day we moved out he collapsed with a massive arterial nosebleed and spent five weeks in hospital, followed by numerous tests. They found that his breathing kept stopping during the night, so in the day it was as if he were climbing Everest without oxygen. After this he used a mask and a massive oxygen machine every night, and started feeling much better.

The specialists hadn't finished with him. Early in 2008 a muscle biopsy proved he had inclusion body myositis, a rare degenerative condition affecting the voluntary muscles, especially the long muscles of the arms and legs. He had probably had it for about seven years. Eventually, they said, it would put him in a wheelchair.

The kind occupational therapist came to work out what equipment he might need, and asked him tactfully whether he might occasionally fix himself a little snack in the kitchen. We both burst out laughing, and explained he'd been used to doing half the cooking. (She was astonished.) The perching stool she sent him didn't help, and soon he knew his cooking days were over. He had no confidence in his ability to manage hot pans or pots of boiling water safely – already his arm and hand muscles were not to be trusted. Nor were his legs, and he had more falls. Even more than cooking, he missed gardening – all he could do was sit outside and supervise Helen, our bright, eager schoolgirl helper, and try not to get too frustrated by my amateur efforts.

That November he had to give up driving as well: his right leg couldn't be relied on to move between the accelerator and the brake. A year later he could no longer manage the stairs, and moved down to the ground-floor bedroom.

It was the first time I'd had to do everything to feed us since he moved in, but I could manage. The real problem was Harvey's lack of enthusiasm. Eating seemed to be turning into simply one more burdensome task he had to get through to stay alive. I would serve him something he liked, sit down with him at the table, and wait hopefully for a comment, which rarely came.

Enjoying the food myself wasn't enough, and his eating so little somehow made me want to eat too much. He had always been so full of vigour and zest for life's pleasures, including cooking and eating. Now I felt guilty relief when I fed guests who eagerly welcomed and dispatched everything I put in front of them.

His was not the worst of fates, or so we told ourselves: although inexorable and untreatable, his illness was slow and painless and did not impair his mind at all. Yet he was unable to manage more than an occasional walk on a good day, down our lane and over the road to the bench outside the dairy. His swallowing was affected, as well as his breathing. His appetite dwindled to the point where I knew he simply wasn't getting enough food, and had to try hard to stop myself going on at him about it and making things worse. We needed help.

Negotiating our way through the healthcare maze took a while, but when we finally got to see the hospital dietitian she supplied exactly what I was sure he needed – two bottles of sweet milky Fortisip a day. The wonderful thing about complete meal supplements like this is that, as nutrition levels are restored, appetite revives, at least a little. Fortunately Harvey had always liked milkshakes so he had no trouble getting down the Fortisip, along with a small bowl of porridge for breakfast and crackers or toast with bits of cheese, pickles and fruit for lunch.

He would eat a small normal dinner, only the main course unless we had visitors. He always had his whisky with the television news first, along with a mini-packet of potato chips: the chips were my idea as he needed the extra salt to offset his medications. He could still manage most of the things he'd always liked best – not just the softer dishes, casseroles, stews and carefully deboned fish, but well-baked pork chops, thin slices of tender roast meat, slim French lamb cutlets, chicken, duck, and even steak, although it had to be fillet.

Oysters were perfect, but he stopped eating flounder because he couldn't lift the flesh off the bones and wouldn't let me do it for him – I don't think he trusted me to get out every bone. Almost every night I made him potatoes, sometimes cooking pasta or rice for myself, or making two different dinners so we could both have what we wanted. He was grateful, but missed being able to consider what to have for dinner.

He wrote in his blog:

One of my big present regrets is that I can no longer cook.
I can still read and drool over recipe books. I can think of
adaptations as I read and can ask Anne to contemplate trying
such and such a dish. But I cannot suddenly ask, 'Would you
like to have this tonight?' While Anne not only has to do all
the meal preparation (and the clearing up), she has to cook
for someone who has little appetite.

Celebrations had to be carefully thought out so Harvey could
enjoy the food and not get too tired, and so I didn't get too
frazzled – I found it a strain to organise a special spread on
top of the regular daily routine of looking after him. And
there was something else I could never talk to him about: I
found holidays and anniversaries hard to enjoy because they
brought home to me how much had changed since he became
ill. But he still wanted to mark such occasions properly, as
we had always done, and I wanted him to feel satisfied with
how we did it.

First we needed to get him a better chair, so he could
stay sitting comfortably at the table for the whole dinner.
His original office chair, made in Wellington by Ergoform,
was the one that suited him best. They made and delivered
another one. For our twenty-fourth wedding anniversary in
2009, we invited five guests for a long lunch. Overcoming my
chronic parsimony, I came up with the idea of commissioning
a caterer, Harriet Harcourt, to deliver two roast ducks with

orange sauce, and a sharp lemon tart, leaving me to make just the easy entrée – one of Harvey's favourites, melon and prosciutto – and a potato gratin, ratatouille and salad.

It worked perfectly. As arranged, Harriet arrived just as we finished the entrée. She'd cooked everything that morning, so it was all fresh. The sauce was a triumph, its juicy little orange segments stripped of pith with a neatness I'd never mastered. I could relax, and Harvey stayed happily in his chair and ate a little of every course.

For his seventy-sixth birthday in 2010, his friend Oliver brought us the most magnificent whitebait I'd ever seen – 500 grams of great big ones with stripes down their backs. A West Coast farmer had caught them in a pair of pantyhose strung across her creek. By then I'd learnt how to cook whitebait his way and produced three large patties – so big that, for the first time in his life, Harvey had more whitebait than he could eat.

Soon Christmas was looming. I worked out a plan I thought would suit both us and our seven guests. Instead of a late lunch we would have an early dinner, giving us a more peaceful morning and letting me put off cooking until after midday. And instead of ducks or the beef fillet I'd resorted to in recent years, this year I would give Harvey back his favourite roast pork.

In November I made the Christmas pudding but not a Christmas cake – unlike most men, Harvey didn't care for it and I wasn't bothered. I'd taken to making a really good gingerbread in December instead, giving us something we both liked and that kept well to serve visitors. By the Wednesday before Christmas we had had so many visitors there wasn't much gingerbread left in the tin. I cut it up carefully and put it out for that afternoon's arrivals, then went out to finish the shopping, knowing Harvey was well looked after. When I came home there were three small pieces left – his visitors had enjoyed it but he hadn't had any. I sat down with him for a late cup of tea and he asked for a piece, then the second and the third. I watched him eat with astonished delight.

It was almost the last thing he ate at home. That night he stayed up later than usual. As I waited to put him to bed, I heard a small noise from his room and went in. He had fallen forward on to his walker, knocking it sideways into his desk and trapping himself.

The ambulance took him to intensive care. The next day he seemed to be rallying well but on Friday, Christmas Eve, he was much weaker, and although he desperately wanted to come home for Christmas we both knew he couldn't. I had already alerted our friends, cancelled my pork order and bought ham instead, and rearranged everything around being with him for much of Christmas Day. Late on Friday afternoon he was moved to a high-monitoring ward and I went home, confident he was in good hands. The last thing he did after I left was tell his best friend where to find my Christmas presents so I could have them to open in the morning.

At 4.20 a.m. the hospital rang. His lungs were failing. He died in the early hours of Christmas Day, as the sky outside was turning deep blue.

10

The next best thing

I spent the afternoon and evening of that Christmas Day with the friends we had invited for dinner. They knew Harvey had died that morning, but I told them I wanted them to come. What else was I going to do that day? They arrived with generous supplies of food and took care of everything, while I sat in Harvey's place at the head of the table, eating and drinking and talking as if it were a normal Christmas, pretending to myself that Harvey was simply in hospital.

Boxing Day was taken up with phone calls and making all the necessary arrangements, but I dreaded the days ahead. Then our friend Ali rang to say she was coming to stay with me for a week, until the private funeral on Friday, December 31. I was grateful for her gentle kindness and quiet competence, but above all for her company and her cooking.

She came laden with the kind of mild food she thought I would feel like – a loaf of her own fine focaccia bread, home-grown tomatoes and artichokes, and a panforte as a late Christmas present. She brought a piquant Elizabeth David cream and white wine sauce she had made to heat up and serve with the ham she knew we would be eating, turning it into a delicate dish with the distinguished name of le saupiquet des Amognes.

After Harvey's funeral my sister and brother-in-law stayed on, getting me through another two days, but after that I had to face eating alone. When Harvey was ill I used to think about what it would be like when I was on my own. I was sure having dinner by myself would be one of the worst things, and I was right. Working out how to manage it proved even harder than I expected.

In 2008 I had started blogging about my life and times on *Elsewoman*, and early in 2009 I helped Harvey set up his own blog, *Stoat Spring*. For two years he posted on it almost every morning. After he died, I used both *Elsewoman* and *Something Else to Eat*, the food blog I had set up in March 2010, to write about coming to terms with my new life as a woman alone.

On January 4 I went to the supermarket for the first time since Harvey died. Ever since I had started shopping and cooking when I married at nineteen, I'd had at least one other person to cook for and eat with. Now all that had vanished.

There were so many things I no longer needed to buy, but when I tried to think what I should buy I had no idea. I wandered round slowly, trying to work out what to do. I knew I had a friend coming for dinner on Wednesday and another one on Friday, so I bought ravioli and chicken. Bread – there was none left. Milk, garlic, wine. That was about it.

I had no intention of betraying the long, deeply pleasurable tradition of cooking and eating well that Harvey and I had built up together by serving myself bad or simply indifferent food, but it was difficult not to get discouraged. Going out to an event starting at five or six and coming home late and hungry to an empty house, it was easy to settle for a tin or a takeaway – there are three takeaway places at the end of my driveway – but whenever I did this it always left me feeling vaguely cheated, and lonelier than usual.

Cooking for myself, once I got used to it, turned out to be a welcome distraction. I found it absorbing, like writing, only easier to do and look forward to, and with a much faster pay-off. It gave me a sense of being taken care of, as I was when Harvey was alive and well. And unlike most of the other kinds of caring, such as being hugged or asked about your day, it was something I could do for myself.

When I'm shopping or cooking, I often talk to myself about what I'm doing. I've always done that, much to Harvey's amusement (and my embarrassment when somebody else caught me at it). I do it more now because the house is so bloody quiet. Music helps, although I'm nowhere near as good or as knowledgeable a listener as Harvey was, and so does the radio, although I hate it just being background noise, like my mother's perpetual 1ZB.

As for food, it took me months to get attuned to what I really wanted to eat. How do I decide now there's only me?

I've had to learn to pick up even faint signals, like a fastidious cat sniffing the morning air. Although those ingrained rules about 'not spending too much' on food have changed and become more flexible over the years, even now they get in the way of tracking down what would suit me best that day.

I still have trouble working out how much to buy and make, but for the most part I've learnt to overcome my old habit of eating more than I need or really want because it's there, I enjoy it, and it's sensual and comforting. The secret seems to be matching what I make as closely as I can to exactly what I feel like having, fully satisfying both my hunger for food and my desire for pleasure, without overdoing it. A little of what you fancy really does do you good.

The supply of recipes is infinite, from my lifelong collection of cookbooks and the well-used folder of Lois Daish columns torn from the *Listener* to my computer file of new ideas downloaded from the internet. But halving or quartering ingredients all the time can get depressing.

The endless barrage of 'reality' food shows doesn't help. If they're not focused on restaurant cooking, with flustered contestants struggling to serve up elaborate food for others, they almost always show happy tables full of chirpy people eagerly awaiting the celebrity cook's masterpiece. When was the last time anyone made a TV show about cooking for one?

It's true that I rarely go to as much trouble for myself alone as I do when I have guests, and some familiar enterprises – roasts, casseroles, lasagne – demand their presence so as not to lead to endless repeats. But I do try new recipes, and work out new ways of combining what's available. Often that includes leftovers from a more ambitious dinner, and their second life can be even better than their first.

Some of the best soups I've made have been concocted from surplus cooked vegetables. Carefully heated up potato gratin is delicious; mashed or boiled potato, fried to a crisp in a little duck fat, is superb. But I've also had to make myself see that, rather than packing all the leftovers tidily away on my hips, it's okay to throw away something that won't freeze well, or wasn't all that nice to start with, or I really don't want to have again, and get something fresh to eat instead – maybe just a poached egg if that's all I fancy.

With only myself to feed, every so often I can lash out on the luxury versions of fast food. A small fillet of pork, beef or salmon, a slim little rack of lamb, a handful of plump scallops, a gleaming creamy-white sole. But humbler things can be equally good: spaghetti carbonara with garlic, bacon, eggs and parmesan; a basic Thai curry, red or green, chicken or prawn, with extra vegetables that don't appear in the genuine version – sliced onions or shallots, corn kernels, diced peppers; eggplant parmigiana, the fleshy slices melting into the garlicky, cheese-topped tomato sauce; a classic Caesar salad made with my own cos leaves; or a salade composée with good blue cheese, a sliced apple or pear and Waikanae friends' walnuts strewn over my own rocket or my new green and purple lettuce, 'Drunken Woman Fringed Head'.

I had already started managing the pot garden and little side patch before Harvey died; now it's all up to me and I can't ask his advice. Fortunately I have the help and encouragement of Ali, a gifted born gardener like him – it was she who found me the Drunken Woman lettuce. Between us we've made sure there'll be no shortage of herbs or salad greens this year. Stepping outside to pick them for dinner, as Harvey used to do, is both sad and comforting.

I don't run to growing asparagus but a neat rank of tender green spears can become my main course, with a soft-boiled egg on top and maybe a little bacon on the side. Even better, when Tony Gamboni of Gamboni's Deli, which opened not long before Harvey died, gave me a bone with plenty of precious prosciutto left on it, I cut the dark rose-coloured meat into little pieces, fried them in butter and scattered them over the top.

No, the food isn't the problem. The problem is how to eat dinner on my own.

To grasp the wrongness of eating alone, all you need to do is Google it. There are scores of sites devoted to reassuring you it's perfectly okay to eat in a restaurant by yourself, or impressing upon you the importance of eating well when you live alone, then explaining how best to accomplish both these difficult feats. The spate of advice merely confirms that, given a choice, most human beings don't want to eat alone. It doesn't suit us, unless we're engaged in a great enterprise such as living in the bush trying to save a rare endangered bird, in which case food is reduced to nothing more than necessary fuel. Even then, few relish the solitude for long.

When it comes to eating alone, breakfast and lunch don't count – it's dinner that matters. Having no one to eat dinner with hammers home the truth: you have no one to share your daily life with.

Admittedly it's a self-centred concern compared with not being able to put enough good food on the table for yourself – or worse, for your children – but it's real for one in four people in New Zealand, and the number is rising. Despite the loving care of her family, my birth mother, Mary, became depressed, stopped feeding herself well, and decided to move into a rest home – not because she couldn't cook for herself, but because she could no longer cope with having no one else to cook for and eat with. Possibly, if I live long enough, I will do the same – cooking for one is an effort and I may grow tired of making it.

I have no family living in Wellington now: my son Jonathan has been teaching in China for nine years. Harvey had no family here either, but we did have friends. On what turned out to be Harvey's last evening at home, our neighbour Frances, a retired historian, came to dinner. After Harvey died I gave her a regular invitation: she comes to dinner once a week for three weeks, and on the fourth week she takes me out. We have a very good time. Last week she told me about a new kind of coffin you can buy in advance and use as a bookcase. We moved on to the problem of buying small amounts of good bread. I suggested she get a breadmaker but she said she had nowhere to put it. 'Maybe,' she said, 'I could put it in the coffin!'

My friends are wonderful and indispensable, yet no matter how close they are, or how much I enjoy their company, they can't fill the gap left by the loss of the man I not only loved but, perhaps even more importantly, really liked and got on with so well for so long.

Some friends who have lived alone for a long time, or at least since their children left home, can be dismissive: 'Well yes, I've been coping on my own for years.' But they started living alone when they were younger and still going out to work, which may have made it a little easier.

When my first husband left, the loneliest times were the evenings after the children had gone to bed. Now I can be alone in various ways without feeling lonely at all – except at dinner time. Each day I plan how to navigate this with as much enjoyment as possible.

I've had to make myself sit at the table for dinner instead of using a tray on my lap. I've worked out I can rearrange the room so I can sit at the side of the table, instead of at the end with the table stretching out forlornly in front of me. It helps to have my place set with a napkin, a glass of wine, and a good water glass. But no matter how good the food is, just sitting there staring into space is not going to work, nor is reading, and sound alone can't dispel the silence. I need faces, the illusion of company.

I turn on the television, searching for something to eat by. It won't be a cooking show – somehow these spoil both the food on the screen and the food on my plate. Nor will it be fast-paced comedy – it's too frenetic, although *Friends* or *The*

Simpsons will do at a pinch. What works best is something familiar but absorbing, and probably old-fashioned: Trollope or Elizabeth Gaskell on DVD. I have to take care not to get so distracted that I eat automatically, not noticing what I'm putting into my mouth, or I come to and realise it's almost all gone and I haven't appreciated it, when that's the whole point.

Here I am, then, leaving the computer and going downstairs to watch the six o'clock news, as we always used to do, with a small plate of something to serve as a starter – a few olives, fresh tomatoes on crackers, a bit of silky, pale green, home-made guacamole, and a glass of tomato juice. (On my own one glass of wine is enough, I tell myself firmly, so most nights I save that for dinner.)

When the sports news comes on, I start cooking. I bought fresh prawn cutlets this morning to have with Tony's tagliatelle, which comes in neat, flat, intricately woven parcels, just right for one. I cook it first, and keep it warm with a little butter stirred through, using the cooking water to warm one of my lovely big deep-rimmed old soup plates. I fry the prawns quickly in butter, take them out of the pan, pour in a little wine or vermouth and reduce it before adding lime juice. The prawns go back to cook gently for a little longer, along with a bit of chilli jam (a present) and some fresh coriander from the garden. I finish off the sauce with cream and turn it out carefully over the pretty pasta ribbons, adding a little more finely chopped coriander and a grinding of black pepper. On the table there's a glass of white wine and a green garden salad. In the pantry there's a piece of goat's cheese left over from dinner with Frances, and there are two chocolates left in the box Ali brought me last week. Dinner for one is not as good as dinner for two who are happy together. But it can be the next best thing.

Recipes

Roast leg of lamb in a mustard coat

With slight adaptations, 'Gigot à la moutarde', from *Mastering the Art of French Cooking, Volume I*, is my favourite recipe for roast lamb, though of course it's not how my mother cooked it. As the authors point out, it does away with the need for high-temperature cooking at the beginning, and 'the lamb becomes a beautiful brown as it roasts'. Serves 6–10, depending on appetites.

> 1 small leg of lamb, about 2.5kg, trimmed of as much fat
>   as possible (for a larger leg, increase the coating recipe)
> a few meaty bones and meat trimmings (a cheap shoulder
>   chop can provide these)
> 1–2 sprigs fresh rosemary
>
> *For the mustard coating*
> 1 teaspoon finely ground rosemary leaves (easiest to do this
>   in a blender)
> 120ml (about ½ cup) Dijon mustard
> 2 tablespoons soy sauce
> 1–2 cloves garlic, mashed
> ¼ teaspoon powdered ginger
> 1 tablespoon extra virgin olive oil
>
> *For the sauce*
> 150ml (approx.) dry white wine

- Remove lamb from the refrigerator at least 3 hours before it needs to go in the oven.

- To ground rosemary leaves, add all other coating ingredients except olive oil. Combine well in a blender or food processor, or beat together by hand. Beat in olive oil drop by drop to make a thickish mayonnaise-like cream.

- Use a soft spatula or brush to paint mustard mixture evenly over lamb, reserving 1–2 tablespoons for the sauce. If you are cooking lamb more than 2 hours later, loosely cover it so as not to disturb the coating and put it back in the refrigerator. Take it out again 1 hour before cooking.

- Preheat oven to 190°C, fan-forced if available. Put meat trimmings, bones and sprigs of rosemary in the bottom of a roasting tin. Place lamb over them on a rack. Turn oven down to 180°C just before putting lamb into the oven.

- Roast lamb until just done to your liking, turning once. (A meat thermometer is a great help. The internal temperature for medium rare is around 155°C. Most books recommend 1 hour per kg, but this requires the meat to be at room temperature, not chilled, when it goes into the oven, and it may still need some extra time.)

- Take lamb out of the oven and rest on a warmed plate, with the bone propped up at an angle so juices run back into the meat, for at least 15 minutes. Cover lightly with a folded tea towel until ready to carve.

- Briefly brown meat trimmings and bones in roasting tin, being careful not to burn them, then remove from tin. Add wine, scrape bits off bottom of tin, and increase heat to reduce wine by about half.

- Stir in reserved mustard coating and about 150ml water. (Or leave coating in the blender, add water, run blender briefly to combine and pour liquid into tin.)

- Deglaze tin and reduce sauce again over medium heat until it is a good pouring consistency. Test for seasoning. Just before serving, reheat and strain into a warmed sauceboat.

Rissoles

This is the most popular recipe on my food blog. Genuine rissoles must be made with cold leftover roast meat. There's no exact recipe, because quantities depend on the amount of meat available. This is how my mother made them from the Sunday roast leftovers, usually hogget or beef. They are equally good made with pork. The crucial thing is to use plenty of seasoning and not to overwhelm the meat with the padding, or the rissoles will be stodgy and dull. Serve with a good home-made chutney, relish, or tomato sauce, a salad, and bread and butter if required.

cold roast meat
cooked potatoes (preferably boiled or mashed) and/or fresh
   breadcrumbs
plain flour (optional)
salt and freshly ground black pepper
1 onion
1 handful assorted fresh herbs, e.g. parsley, thyme, oregano
   (if fresh herbs are not available, use dried)
1–2 cloves garlic (optional)
1–2 eggs
a little stock, wine or water to mix if required
flour for coating

- Cut up into chunks all the cold meat you want to use, taking care to remove any solid pieces of fat, scraps of bone and pieces of gristle. Mince meat in a food processor until well ground but still dry, and place in a large bowl.

- Add some form of carbohydrate – approximately half as much as there is meat. You can use leftover cooked potato or fresh breadcrumbs (made in the processor after you remove the meat) or a combination of both with a little flour. Mix all together well, with plenty of salt and pepper.

- Using the pulse button, finely chop onion (small or large, depending on how much mixture you have), herbs and garlic (if using) together in the processor. Add all this to mixture.

- Break in 1 egg (or 2 eggs for a large amount) and mix all together gently but thoroughly. If one egg leaves mixture a little too dry and crumbly, add a little stock, wine or water, taking care not to make it too wet. The mixture should just hold together enough to be shaped into balls about the size of a large mandarin. Use damp hands to do this.

- Flatten each ball to make a round patty about 1.5cm thick. Spread a thin layer of flour over a plate and coat each patty lightly with flour on each side. If possible, set rissoles aside to rest, well spread out on a large flat plate or board, for approximately 10 minutes before cooking.

- Set oven to 100°C and put a large metal oven tray in to warm, with a double layer of kitchen paper on it to absorb any excess oil. Coat a wide frypan lightly with a shallow layer of oil and heat until ready for gentle frying.

- Cook rissoles over medium heat in batches, leaving space around each one (usually 5 or 6 will fit into a large pan). When one side is starting to become brown and a little crispy, turn and cook the other side. Add more oil if needed between batches. As each batch cooks, put them on the tray in the oven to keep warm.

Rich Christmas pudding

This should be made at least a month before Christmas. My mother used this recipe – the only thing missing is the silver threepences. It originally appeared in the *Edmonds Cook Book* as 'Christmas Pudding (Rich)', but it had disappeared by the mid 1980s. The slightly odd repeated measure of 125 grams was originally 4 ounces. You will need a traditional metal pudding basin with a lid and a large lidded saucepan to steam it in. The standing overnight is essential. Blue flames should be licking around the pudding as it is brought to the table. For brandy sauce, make a classic smooth, buttery, flowing white sauce without seasoning, and add brown sugar and brandy to taste. Serves at least 8.

50g plain flour
125g fresh soft white breadcrumbs
125g brown sugar
125g suet, grated (Shreddo, which appears in supermarkets
    around November)
125g apple, peeled and chopped
125g raisins
125g sultanas
125g currants (you can replace half or all the currants with
    dried cranberries and/or finely chopped dried apricots)
50g whole unpeeled almonds
25g mixed peel
zest of 1 large lemon
½ teaspoon nutmeg
½ teaspoon allspice or mixed spice
¼ teaspoon salt
2 large eggs
juice of ½ lemon
2 tablespoons brandy
3 more tablespoons brandy for Christmas Day

- Put sifted flour, breadcrumbs, sugar and suet into a large mixing basin. Add apple, dried fruit, almonds, peel and lemon rind, then spices and salt. Mix gently.

- Beat eggs well and add them with lemon juice. Stir well to mix. (Everyone in the house should have a stir at this point, for good luck in the New Year.)

- Cover bowl and leave to stand overnight.

- Next day, lightly butter pudding basin. Stir first 2 tablespoons of brandy into the mixture, place in basin, press down slightly to level it, and put lid on firmly.

- Put enough water in a large saucepan to come halfway up the sides of pudding basin (test level before heating water). Bring water to a gentle continuous boil. Stand pudding basin in water and cover everything with a well-fitting lid. Turn heat down until water is bubbling very gently.

- Steam pudding for 4 hours, making sure water stays at a very gentle bubbling boil. Check water level after 2 hours and add enough boiling water to keep level roughly halfway up basin.

- Turn off heat and leave to stand for another hour. Take out pudding in its basin and leave in refrigerator.

- On Christmas Day, open basin lid and pour 1 tablespoon brandy over pudding. Replace lid and steam pudding for another 2 hours.

- Turn off heat and carefully remove hot basin. Grasping it in a thick tea towel, remove lid. Hold a warm serving platter, larger than top of basin and preferably with a small rim, firmly over the top and turn everything over. Tap firmly all over bottom of basin and shake it gently. The pudding should then turn out whole.

- To flame pudding, gently heat last 2 tablespoons brandy, pour over and light.

Proper trifle

In my opinion jelly has no place in a proper trifle, but sherry is essential – I prefer medium to sweet. The trifle sponge needs to be dry and I buy it, as my mother did. Dark berries are the best fruit to use because their colour and sharpness contrast so well with the sponge, custard and cream. My mother used custard powder but real egg custard tastes better. The cornflour in the recipe prevents the custard curdling and makes it slightly thicker, though it's still thinner and lighter than the ready-made custard alternative. You can add fresh fruit or nuts, e.g. slivered almonds, to decorate the top, but I prefer it left plain. Each serving should have as even a share as possible of all the layers. If you have suitable bowls you can also make individual trifles.

For the custard
6 large egg yolks
1 tablespoon cornflour
750ml standard milk
2–4 tablespoons sugar (depending how sweet you like it)
1 large vanilla pod, split, or 2 teaspoons vanilla essence

◆ Beat yolks with a fork. Mix cornflour with a little cold milk in a small bowl.

◆ Pour milk into a saucepan which can fit well over another pan of water. Add vanilla and sugar. Heat slowly to boiling point, stirring with a wooden spoon.

◆ Remove from heat and take out vanilla pod. Pour milk onto yolks, stirring well. Add cornflour mixed with milk and stir well.

◆ Return mixture to pan and heat over simmering water, stirring gently, until it thickens and coats the back of a wooden spoon, and there is no taste of cornflour.

- Pour into a jug and cool thoroughly before using, with a piece of cling-film pressed down onto the surface of the custard to prevent skin forming.

For the trifle
700g dark berries, one kind or mixed, fresh or frozen
caster sugar to taste
1 large trifle sponge
6 tablespoons medium sherry
700ml custard, home-made or bought
300ml cream
deep glass serving bowl (preferably with a wide base, so that the sponge at the bottom is a similar width to the other layers)

- If using frozen berries, take out ahead of time and defrost before using.

- Place berries in a wide shallow dish. Sprinkle with enough sugar to achieve desired level of sweetness. (Slightly tart berries taste better.) Leave for 1 hour.

- If there is more than ½ cup juice, drain and reduce carefully over a high heat, pour it back over berries and cool thoroughly.

- At least 2 hours ahead of serving, break sponge into rough squares and fit into as even a layer as possible in base of serving bowl. Sprinkle evenly with sherry and leave for 1 hour.

- Cover sponge with a thick layer of berries and juice, then a thick layer of custard.

- Cover with cling-film and leave in refrigerator.

- Take out 30 minutes before serving. Just before serving, whip cream and spread evenly over custard.

Seventeenth-century pork chops

This recipe came from my friend Frances, who gave me my first cooking lessons. If you wish you can bake two large oval Agria potatoes, well-scrubbed, halved horizontally, brushed with oil and sprinkled with salt, on a lower rack at the same time. Serve with salad or green beans. Serves 2.

1 small onion
2 tablespoons parsley
2 teaspoons lemon juice
3 tablespoons olive oil
salt and freshly ground black pepper
2 large pork chops

• Peel onion and grate it into a small bowl. Finely chop parsley and add it to onion. Add lemon juice and 2 tablespoons of the olive oil. Season with salt and pepper and mix well.

• At least 1 hour and up to 10 hours before cooking, brush one side of chops with the remaining 1 tablespoon olive oil and place them in a shallow ceramic baking dish, oiled side down. (You can also use a metal dish – this speeds up cooking but can also dry chops out.) Spread onion mixture over their upper sides. Leave in refrigerator until 30 minutes before cooking.

• Preheat oven to 180°C. Place baking dish on shelf in middle of oven. Bake chops for approximately 1 hour, until topping is browned a little and a thin knife slides easily into the meat. Lift out and rest on kitchen paper for 10 minutes before serving.

American baked cheesecake

This came from Augusta and Bob Ford. The original recipe required Zwieback toasts and ¼ cup of sugar for the crust. Plain digestive biscuits are the best New Zealand replacement, and do not require added sugar. Serve with a little softly whipped cream, nothing else. Serves 8–10.

For the crust
250g plain digestive biscuits
115g butter, softened

* Turn biscuits into coarse crumbs by putting them into a plastic bag and crushing with a rolling pin, or whizzing briefly in a food processor. Pick out any larger pieces. Put crumbs in a large bowl and work in soft butter.

* Lightly butter a large, round, deep, loose-bottomed cake tin and cover base with baking paper. Press crumb mixture over base and sides to form a shell of even thickness. Put tin in refrigerator to harden while you prepare filling.

For the filling
250g plain cottage cheese
250g cream cheese (not spreadable or light)
2 large eggs
1 cup white sugar
2 tablespoons cornflour
pinch of salt
250g sour cream
200ml standard milk
1 teaspoon natural vanilla essence
cream to serve

- Heat oven to 180°C.
- In a large bowl, beat cottage cheese and cream cheese together. Lightly beat 1 egg and add it to cheeses. Beat second egg and add it.
- In a separate bowl, mix together sugar, cornflour and salt, and stir thoroughly into cheese and egg mixture.
- Stir in sour cream, milk and vanilla essence.
- Pour loose batter carefully into hardened shell in cake tin. Bake for 1 hour, until filling is set. Turn oven off and leave cheesecake in it to cool for 1 hour.
- Take cheesecake out of oven and leave to cool to room temperature.
- For serving, carefully remove ring of cake tin. Gently slide entire cheesecake, with baking paper under it, off base of cake tin onto serving plate.
- For serving next day, keep cheesecake in cake tin and store in refrigerator overnight, covered with a loose plastic bag. Remove in time to bring it up to room temperature.

Chicken stuffed with fruits

This is one of the first recipes I made from Claudia Roden's *A Book of Middle Eastern Food*. I like this mix of fruits – the original recipe also includes raisins. I use the second cooking method, where the chicken is wrapped. As Roden says, this makes it 'more tender and juicy'. Good accompaniments are a bowl of plain yoghurt and a plain rice pilaf. Serve Middle Eastern salads as a first course. Serves 4–6.

> 1 large roasting chicken
> 1 large onion, finely chopped
> butter for cooking
> 200g dried prunes, soaked, stoned and chopped
> 350g dried apricots, soaked, stoned and chopped
>   (New Zealand ones are by far the best)
> 2 medium tart apples, peeled, cored and chopped
> salt and freshly ground black pepper
> 1 teaspoon ground cinnamon
> 1 teaspoon ground sumac

- Preheat oven to 180°C. (If using fan forced, you may need to lower the temperature to 170°C.)

- Fry onion in 2 tablespoons hot butter until soft and golden. Add fruits and sauté gently for a few minutes. Season to taste with salt, pepper, cinnamon and sumac. Sauté gently for a minute or two longer.

- Empty chicken cavity if necessary, wash chicken and wipe it dry inside and out. Stuff chicken with fruit mixture. Rub with salt and pepper and tie it up neatly.

- Place in a roasting dish. Turn oven down to 160°C. Roast for approximately 25 minutes per 500g. Baste frequently with melted butter.

- Alternatively, cover chicken in butter shavings and wrap in foil or in a large roasting oven bag, including any leftover stuffing.

- Place in roasting dish and cook at 180°C for 20 minutes per 500g. Check to ensure chicken is thoroughly cooked through and cook for longer if necessary. At the end of cooking, carefully drain any liquid from the parcel before completely unwrapping and serving.

Orange and almond cake

Adapted from *A Book of Middle Eastern Food*, by Claudia Roden, this is a Sephardic cake, a traditional recipe from the Jewish communities who lived in Spain and Portugal until the Spanish Inquisition drove them away to the Middle East. Roden says it never fails, and in my experience she's right. It's so moist that if you want to keep it for more than a day or two, it needs to go in the refrigerator. Serve with a little softly whipped cream or with yoghurt. If you like, you can add a little orange liqueur or orange blossom water to the accompanying cream when you whip it. Thick creamy Greek-style yoghurt is very good too – or nothing at all, just the cake. Serves 6–8.

> 2 large oranges
> 6 eggs
> 250g ground almonds
> 250g white sugar
> 1 teaspoon baking powder
> butter and flour for cake tin
> cream or plain unsweetened yoghurt to serve

- Wash oranges and boil gently in a little water in a lidded saucepan for nearly 2 hours, until they are soft. Check every 30 minutes to see if they need a little more water. (You can boil the oranges the day or the morning before making the cake.)

- Remove oranges from saucepan, let them cool, then cut them open and remove pips. Turn the whole oranges, including the skin, into a pulp, either by rubbing through a sieve or by pulsing in an electric blender or food processor.

- Heat oven to 190°C. (If you have an oven with a fan, do not use it – use the bake setting.) Butter and flour a round loose-bottomed cake tin.

- Beat eggs in a large bowl. Add all other ingredients in order given, and mix thoroughly. (I pour the beaten eggs into the orange pulp in the food processor bowl and add the other ingredients one at a time, whizzing just enough to mix well after each one and scraping down the bowl carefully between each addition. The baking powder should be added last, using a small sieve, to make sure it's evenly distributed.)

- Pour carefully into cake tin and bake for approximately 1 hour. If it is still very wet, leave in oven for a little longer. A thin skewer poked into the middle should come out almost clean when cake is done. Leave to cool in tin before turning out.

Speca te mbushura – stuffed peppers

This is a lighter, easier, faster version than the stuffed vegetables Rosia made for us in Albania, but it tastes the same. Serves 4.

1 medium onion, finely chopped
3 tablespoons olive oil
200g lean beef, finely minced
1 tin crushed Italian tomatoes
1 tablespoon parsley, finely chopped
1 teaspoon marjoram, finely chopped
1 cup cooked long grain rice
salt and freshly ground black pepper
4 large red, yellow or orange peppers

* Preheat oven to 180°C.

* Gently fry onion in 2 tablespoons oil until it softens. Add minced beef and fry gently until it changes colour.

* Add ½ tin of tomatoes and all other ingredients except peppers. Mix well and simmer gently for 10 minutes. Check seasoning and leave to cool a little.

* Carefully cut tops out of peppers. Remove seeds and white pith through the hole.

* Place peppers with 1 tablespoon oil in a shallow glass or ceramic dish just large enough to hold them. Microwave until they have begun to soften.

* Fill each pepper with meat mixture and arrange in ceramic dish.

* Add ½ cup water and some salt and pepper to remaining ½ tin of tomatoes. Pour this liquid around peppers. Bake for 30 minutes, checking to see that liquid has not dried out.

Mish me kos – meat with yoghurt

Also known as tave Elbasan – the dish of Elbasan. Serves 4–6.

1kg lean lamb pieces or small lean lamb chops
150g butter
100g flour
700g plain thick yoghurt
4 large eggs
salt and freshly ground black pepper
1 cup cooked long-grain rice (optional)
1 tablespoon extra butter

- Preheat oven to 190°C.

- Put meat in shallow frypan and just cover with water. Season with salt. Simmer meat gently until just cooked through. Remove the meat and set aside. Reserve the water.

- In a saucepan, melt the butter. Remove from heat and quickly stir in the flour. Return to low heat for a few minutes, stirring constantly. Remove from heat and quickly stir in the reserved cooking water to make a smooth sauce. Cook gently for a few minutes to thicken. Stir in the yoghurt and cook briefly. Beat the eggs and add to the sauce off the heat. Check seasoning.

- Put meat in one layer in wide ceramic dish. Add rice to make a more substantial dish. Pour sauce over the top. Dot top with butter.

- Place in upper half of oven. Bake for 15–20 minutes until a crust forms on top of the sauce.

Revised ratatouille

The classic ratatouille is superb, but requires a large amount of olive oil. This is my lighter version. It fulfils Julia Child's cardinal principle for this dish: cook each vegetable separately first, then combine them briefly, to keep the true flavours. If you grow your own tomatoes or can get really good quality fresh ones, use these instead of or in addition to the tinned ones. Ratatouille is best served at the temperature the French call tiède, definitely warm but not hot. Serve on its own with crusty bread, or as a vegetable with lamb or beef fillet. Serves 4–6 as a main dish or 6–8 as an entrée or side dish.

> 6 small or 4 medium courgettes
> 1 large eggplant
> 2–3 large, well-ripened sweet peppers – red, orange, yellow, or all three
> 3 medium white or red onions
> 2 cloves New Zealand garlic
> good extra virgin olive oil
> flat-leafed parsley, chopped
> 2 tins Italian crushed tomatoes
> salt and freshly ground black pepper
> 1 teaspoon sugar

- Cut the ends off the courgettes and slice them lengthwise in long even strips, 4–6 strips per courgette (depending how thick they are). Prepare the eggplant the same way, but slice each strip in three lengthwise.

- Put these two vegetables in separate bowls and sprinkle with salt. Set aside while you prepare the other vegetables.

- Remove the tops, white bits and seeds from the peppers and slice them in long even strips no more than 1cm wide.

- Hold a mouthful of water in your mouth while you deal with the onions. Peel, slice off top and bottom, and cut in half vertically. Cut each half onion into thin slices from top to bottom, or push each half onion down, side first, through slicer blade on food processor. Finely chop the garlic.

- Put the onions and garlic and 1 tablespoon oil into a wide shallow ceramic or glass dish, and cover for the microwave. Cook for a few minutes until just tender (I use the 'fresh veges' setting). Remove from dish and set aside.

- Use the same dish, with another tablespoon oil, to cook the peppers using the same method until they are softened but not limp. Remove from dish and set aside.

- Drain and rinse courgettes and cook briefly in the same dish, without adding more oil. They should be just cooked, not limp. Again, remove and set aside.

- Repeat with eggplant. The ratatouille can be made in advance to this point.

- Gently heat a large, preferably non-stick, deep frypan and add another tablespoon oil. Put in each vegetable in alternate layers, sprinkling a little chopped parsley over each layer.

- Add enough peeled and crushed tomatoes to provide moisture and a good balance of flavours. Add 1 teaspoon sugar, freshly ground black pepper and salt to taste. Cook gently for 10 minutes, check seasoning, turn off the heat and leave in pan to cool slightly before serving.

Tarte au fromage

The pastry recipe for this tart is the easiest and most successful savoury short pastry I know. This recipe makes a small tart – double it for a large one. Serves 3 for lunch.

For the pastry
180g flour
½ teaspoon salt
90g butter
2–4 tablespoons iced water

• Preheat oven to 200°C (bake, not fan).

• Rub butter into sieved flour and salt to resemble breadcrumbs. Add enough iced water to form into a ball.

• Do not knead or roll the pastry. Spread it directly into a 23cm flat pie or flan tin with your hands, pressing it lightly into place with your knuckles.

• Prick the base evenly with a fork. Cover pastry with a square piece of baking paper large enough to stick up above the tin at the corners. Chill in refrigerator for 15 minutes.

• Cover paper with dry beans or ceramic baking beads. Bake for 15 minutes. Remove from oven and lift out baking paper with beans or beads inside it. Bake for another 5 minutes (watch to make sure pastry does not darken). Take out of oven while you make the filling.

For the filling
30g butter
2 tablespoons flour
150ml milk, warmed
freshly ground black pepper

cayenne pepper
nutmeg
75g grated gruyère cheese
25g grated parmesan cheese
2 large eggs
cream or milk to brush pastry case

- Heat oven to 200°C (on bake, no fan).

- Separate eggs, putting yolks into a small bowl and whites into a larger bowl.

- Make a stiff béchamel sauce: melt butter in a medium saucepan. Off the heat, rapidly stir in flour. Cook for 2 minutes. Off the heat, add warmed milk, stirring vigorously.

- Season with pepper, cayenne and a grating of nutmeg. Cook on low heat, stirring constantly, until well cooked and reduced. Stir in 60g gruyère cheese and 15–20g parmesan cheese.

- Remove pan from heat. Beat egg yolks very well and stir into sauce. Set aside to cool.

- Beat egg whites until stiff. Fold carefully into sauce.

- Pour filling immediately into pastry case. Brush edges of case with cream or milk. Sprinkle top of filling with remaining cheeses.

- Place tart in oven and bake for 12–15 minutes, until filling is risen and golden brown, but still a little creamy inside. Serve immediately.

Rabbit with mustard and verjus

I used to buy Chinese rabbit in London because it was cheap, but in Wellington Harvey and I would sometimes be able to get a whole one. We each had our own ways of cooking it. I found this delectable recipe in Stephanie Alexander's sumptuous book, *Cooking and Travelling in South-West France*, which Harvey brought home from Unity Books. I've condensed it a little, and I prefer to leave the grapes out. Stephanie Alexander suggests adding tiny new potatoes at the same time as the stock, and including some diced pork fat or pork rind if you're using wild rabbit. You can also make this with chicken or veal. You will need a wide, lidded cooking pot suitable for browning the meat pieces on top of the stove as well as for longer cooking and serving at the table.

1.5kg farmed rabbit cut into pieces
2 tablespoons rendered duck fat
freshly ground black pepper
1 tablespoon mustard of your choice
2 cloves garlic, chopped
100ml verjus
200ml chicken stock
1 cup grapes, seeded (optional)
sea salt
2 tablespoons young flat-leaf parsley, finely chopped

- Trim rabbit pieces neatly, removing belly flaps and bony tail end (use for stock).

- Heat duck fat in dish and thoroughly brown rabbit pieces. Pour off excess fat and grind pepper generously over meat.

- Stir in the mustard.

- After a few minutes, add garlic. Stir until the aroma rises, but do not let it brown.

- Trickle in the verjus on high heat so that it bubbles up and reduces quickly. Stir in stock and lower heat. (Add grapes if using.)

- Press a piece of baking paper over meat and cover with a lid. Simmer gently for 20–25 minutes until tender.

- Remove rabbit to warm dish. Increase heat and boil juices to reduce by half. Taste for seasoning and add salt if necessary. Stir in parsley.

- Return rabbit to pot and stir to coat well with sauce. Serve immediately.

Fudge cake

I found Mum's original handwritten recipe for this recently. It's headed 'Floss Fudge Bix – very good'. Floss was my father's sister. The recipe my birth mother Mary gave me is exactly the same, except that she added chopped ginger. I've increased the quantity of cocoa, because the original 1 tablespoon made a very pale fudge cake – perhaps cocoa was darker in the 1950s.

> 250g wine biscuits or arrowroot biscuits
> 125g butter, softened
> ½ cup sugar
> 1 egg
> 2–3 tablespoons cocoa powder
> 1 teaspoon vanilla essence
> crystallised ginger, nuts and/or dried fruit, chopped (to taste)

- Grease or line with baking paper a shallow oblong tin and set aside.

- Put biscuits into a plastic bag and crush carefully with a rolling pin into little pieces (not crumbs).

- Put butter and sugar into a medium saucepan and heat gently, stirring, until butter is melted.

- Beat egg and cocoa together and add to butter and sugar. Add vanilla essence. Bring just to boil but do not boil.

- Take off heat and add crushed biscuits.

- Add small pieces of ginger, nuts and/or dried fruit as desired.

- Spread mixture in tin and allow to set. Using a sharp knife, cut into small bars and store in an airtight container.

Fresh courgette salad

This is best made with a handful of baby courgettes from the garden, but small fresh bought ones will work. Harvey found the idea as a footnote to Claudia Roden's recipe in *The Food of Italy* for fried courgette salad. He sliced them into rounds, but I think the ribbons look prettier.

4–6 small courgettes
1 tablespoon balsamic vinegar
2 tablespoons good extra virgin olive oil (the better the oil, the better this tastes)
2 cloves garlic, finely chopped
small bunch fresh mint, finely chopped
salt and freshly ground black pepper

- Top and tail the courgettes, but do not peel them. Slice them as thinly as possible, either into rounds, using a food processor slicing blade if available, or lengthwise into long ribbons, using a potato peeler.

- Mix all the other ingredients together to make the dressing.

- Pour dressing over the courgettes, turn to coat thoroughly, and leave for 15–30 minutes before serving.

Duck terrine

The first time Harvey roasted ducks for Christmas, I made this on Boxing Day, using a recipe for chicken terrine found in a timely present from friends: *The World's Finest Chicken*, by Sonia Silver and Janis Metcalfe. Delicious with quince paste and toast.

220g chicken livers
90g dry breadcrumbs
300g leftover cooked duck (or chicken), minced
50g leftover stuffing, preferably made with walnuts (if no stuffing is available, use more duck and/or chicken)
2 large garlic cloves, crushed
1 teaspoon whole black peppercorns
1 tablespoon brandy
1 tablespoon port
1 teaspoon fresh oregano, finely chopped
1 teaspoon fresh rosemary, finely chopped
1 tablespoon fresh flat-leafed parsley, finely chopped
1 large egg, lightly beaten
4–6 rashers bacon, preferrably streaky

• Preheat oven to 190°C.

• Coarsely chop chicken livers. Place in a bowl with breadcrumbs and knead until the mixture forms a ball.

• Add meat, stuffing if using, garlic, peppercorns, brandy, port, herbs and egg. Combine well.

• Use bacon rashers to line the base and sides of an oval ceramic terrine dish or loaf tin (approximately 25cm long, 15cm wide, 6cm deep).

• Spread mixture evenly over bacon lining, and smooth the top. Cover with a tightly fitting lid or aluminium foil (I put foil between the dish and the lid to get a good seal).

- Boil a jugful of water. Place terrine in a large roasting or baking dish. Add enough hot water to come about two-thirds up the sides of terrine. Transfer carefully to the oven and bake for 1¼ hours.

- Remove lid and carefully pour off any liquid fat. Cover and refrigerate overnight. Take out an hour ahead of serving.

Stufatino alla Romana – Roman beef stew

Harvey's favourite beef casserole, this is an excellent slow cooker recipe. It comes from my battered 35-year-old copy of Ada Boni's classic *Talisman Italian Cookbook*, my first introduction to real Italian cooking – before I'd produced only the vaguest of imitations, such as scone-dough pizza. However you cook this, there should not be much sauce, and it should be 'dark and very savoury'. Ada Boni recommends braised celery with the stew, but I like mashed potato and whatever other vegetables you fancy, though Italians probably wouldn't serve any with it. Serves 4.

> 1 onion, cut into small but not tiny pieces
> 2–4 cloves of garlic, chopped
> 1 tablespoon olive oil
> 50g lean bacon, cut into small pieces (the best kind is the solid lump of bacon you can buy from some specialty suppliers, but ordinary bacon is fine)
> 700g cross-cut blade or gravy beef, cut into 2cm cubes
> salt and freshly ground pepper
> 1 tablespoon fresh oregano, chopped
> 250ml (1/3 bottle) robust red wine
> 1 tablespoon tomato paste

Hob or oven method

- Use a shallow, lidded casserole dish that can be placed directly on the heat. If using your oven, set to 180°C, or 170°C on fan forced.

- Sauté the onion and garlic gently in the oil until slightly browned. Add bacon and fry briefly. Add beef with salt, pepper and oregano and let brown gently.

- When beef is well browned, pour wine over and cook until liquid is reduced by half.

- Add tomato paste. Add just enough hot water to cover meat mixture.
- Cover and cook for at least 2 hours, on very low heat on the hob (you will need a metal simmer mat for gas) or on a rack set below the middle of the oven. Check once or twice to see if sauce is becoming too thick and sticky, and add a little more water if necessary.

Slow cooker method

- Set slow cooker to high.
- Combine and cook ingredients as above, using a frypan, but do not add water at the end. Transfer meat mixture into slow cooker dish and add a very small amount of water if it looks too dry. Cook for approximately 4–5 hours on high, checking after 3 hours to see if a little more water needs to be added.

Prunes in tamarillo and chocolate syrup

This is a Lois Daish recipe from her *New Zealand Listener* column about fruit syrups, 5 July 1997. Harvey adored tamarillos, and the combination of that distinctive sharp flavour with the port and chocolate is amazing. You can leave out the prunes and just make the syrup to serve with ice cream or thick yoghurt. Serves 2–3.

2 tamarillos
½ cup water
¼ cup sugar
splash of port or marsala
1 tablespoon cocoa powder
12 pitted prunes

• Plunge tamarillos into a pot of boiling water, leave for a minute, then drain and peel. Slice finely and put in a pot with water, sugar and port or marsala.

• Simmer for 10 minutes, then strain syrup into a bowl through a sieve. Press half the tamarillo pulp through the sieve into syrup.

• Put cocoa in a small pot and gradually stir in syrup. Bring to the boil and add prunes. Simmer for 5 minutes, then leave to steep for several hours.

• Reheat and serve warm with vanilla ice cream.

Mushrooms and bacon

I introduced Harvey to creamed mushrooms, and this used to be one of our favourite weekend breakfasts. After he became ill we would sometimes have it for a light dinner with a bit of fried potato, and I still do this on my own. Serves 2.

4 large flat mushrooms
about 450ml (1½ cups) milk
30g butter
30g plain white flour
salt and freshly ground black pepper
nutmeg
splash of brandy (optional)
4 rashers streaky bacon
good bread for toast
butter for toast

• Remove tough ends of stalks from mushrooms. Cut mushrooms into chunks (roughly 2cm square). Place in ceramic or glass microwave dish, cover, and microwave for 1–2 minutes on medium high to soften them. (This step can be left out, but it is faster and helps commercially grown mushrooms to cook more easily in the sauce later.) Set aside.

• Heat milk in a large glass jug in the microwave, in 30-second bursts on high, until close to boiling (watch it).

• Melt butter in medium heavy-bottomed saucepan over the lowest possible heat. Take off the heat and rapidly stir in flour, using a wooden spoon. Return to heat and cook gently, stirring all the time to avoid lumps, until (says Julia Child) 'the butter and flour froth together for 2 minutes without colouring'.

• Take pan off the heat and slowly pour in 1 cup hot milk, stirring continuously. Put pan back on low heat and cook mixture gently, stirring all the time, until it thickens to a smooth sauce. If it seems to be getting too thick, add more milk, a little at a time (but see note about mushroom juice below).

- Add mushrooms and any juice with them (if they've been microwaved), then add salt to taste. The thickening of the base sauce as it cooks is diluted by the mushroom juices being released. If sauce becomes too thick, add a little more milk.

- Grind in a little black pepper and finely grated nutmeg. Add, if you wish, a small splash of brandy. Cook for a few minutes more, until mushrooms are tender and sauce is dark. Check seasoning.

- Meanwhile heat frypan and gently fry bacon rashers.

- Turn off heat under both pans. Warm plates. Make toast with any good bread, and butter it hot. Gently reheat mushrooms, and serve on toast with rashers alongside.

Roast pork

When Harvey could no longer manage a roast and I had to take over, I found this recipe from the Mad Butcher online and adapted it slightly. Harvey was impressed. The leaves and apple slices seem to keep the meat beautifully moist as it cooks. I collect the apple slices and serve them with the meat. I make the gravy in the roasting pan with white wine and a dash of soy sauce.

2–3kg pork roast, bone in (the exact cut is not important
   but it should have a layer of skin and fat on top)
½ cup olive oil
salt
1 tablespoon fresh sage, finely chopped
¼ cup fresh oregano, finely chopped
¼ cup fresh parsley, finely chopped
3–4 small branches sage leaves
1–2 small branches bay leaves
1–2 apples, cored, unpeeled and sliced

* Preheat oven to 170°C.

* Weigh the pork roast and calculate the cooking time – an hour for every kilogram, plus half an hour. If a meat thermometer is available, insert it into the thickest part of the meat, taking care not to let it touch the bone. Score the rind for crackling.

* Massage roast all over with olive oil, then salt and chopped herbs.

* Put branches of sage, branches of bay leaves and sliced apples on a rack in a roasting pan. Place the roast on top, with the fat uppermost. The Mad Butcher points out that 'The rack keeps the roast out of the drippings, allows the fat to drain away as it melts, and gives better heat circulation around the meat.'

- Place roast in oven and turn oven down to 160°C. Cook the pork roast until the juices run clear when meat is pierced. For pork, the meat thermometer should read 71°C for 'medium' and 76°C for 'well done'.

- Remove the roast and rest in a warm place for 10–30 minutes before carving, covered with a folded tea towel.

Esther's gingerbread

This recipe was given to me by Beth Hill. Electronic scales are useful for it – you can put the bowl and saucepan on them and weigh the ingredients as you go. This keeps very well in an airtight container.

280g flour
200g brown sugar
1 teaspoon baking soda
1 teaspoon baking powder
2 dessertspoons powdered ginger
½ teaspoon mixed spice
½ teaspoon ground nutmeg
1 teaspoon ground cinnamon
225g butter
360g golden syrup
2 eggs
250ml milk

+ Preheat oven to 150°C (bake not fan). Line a 23cm square baking tin with baking paper coming up over the sides a little, so the gingerbread can be lifted out easily when cooked.

+ Into a large bowl, sift flour, brown sugar, baking soda, baking powder and spices.

+ Dice butter and melt with golden syrup in a small saucepan. Add to dry ingredients.

+ Lightly beat eggs and add to mixture. Add milk. Mix well, using a whisk. Pour into prepared tin. (The mixture will be very wet.)

+ Cook for 45–50 minutes, until a skewer inserted into the middle comes out clean.

+ Leave to cool in tin for at least 30 minutes before lifting out onto a rack.

Saupiquet des Amognes –
Ham or smoked chicken with piquant cream sauce

This unusual dish, from Elizabeth David's *French Provincial Cooking*, is 'a modernised version of a famous, very old speciality of the Nivernais and Morvan districts of Burgundy … the sauce should be a beautiful pale coffee-cream colour, smooth but not very thick.' Ali brought this to go with my Christmas ham when she came to stay after Harvey died. Later we made it again with smoked chicken, and that was delicious too. The sauce can be kept and reheated when required. Good with small boiled new potatoes. Serves 3–4.

250ml clear, well-flavoured beef stock
4 shallots, very finely chopped
2–3 crushed juniper berries
6 tablespoons red wine vinegar
2 tablespoons butter
2 tablespoons flour
6 tablespoons white wine
salt and freshly ground black pepper
190ml fresh cream
butter to finish sauce
250g thickly sliced cooked ham or smoked chicken

• Warm stock in glass jug in microwave.

• Put shallots in small saucepan with juniper berries and vinegar. Bring to boil and cook until vinegar has all but evaporated.

• In another saucepan, over a very low heat, melt 2 tablespoons butter, stir in flour and continue stirring until mixture is smooth and turns a pale coffee colour.

- Slowly pour in warmed stock while stirring constantly. Keep stirring until mixture thickens. Add white wine and the shallot mixture. Cook gently for about 30 minutes until all taste of flour has disappeared, removing any scum that comes to the surface.

- Heat oven to 180°C or 170°C fan-forced.

- Sieve the sauce into a clean pan and taste for seasoning. Heat cream (in another pan or in microwave) until just bubbling. Stir into sauce with a small lump of butter.

- Lay overlapping slices of ham or chicken in a shallow ceramic baking dish. Pour over the hot sauce. Heat on shelf around middle of oven, uncovered, for 10–15 minutes.

Parmigiana di melanzane –
Eggplant baked with tomatoes and cheese

This is my lighter version of Claudia Roden's recipe from *The Food of Italy*. To keep it lighter still, grill the eggplant without oil and replace mozzarella with cottage cheese. Serves 2, but can easily be upsized.

   1 large eggplant or 2 medium ones
   olive oil
   1 clove garlic, crushed
   1 tin crushed Italian tomatoes
   1 teaspoon sugar
   salt and freshly ground black pepper
   small bunch basil or mint leaves, chopped
   200–250g mozzarella cheese, diced, or 250g plain cottage cheese
   4 tablespoons grated parmesan cheese

+ Preheat oven to 180°C (fan-forced if available). Slice the eggplants lengthwise, giving slices approximately ½cm thick. Place slices in a large shallow dish, sprinkle with salt and leave for half an hour.

+ Rinse and drain the slices, dry, brush lightly with olive oil, spread over grill rack and grill on each side until lightly browned. Drain on absorbent paper. (For a lighter version, grill them without the oil.)

+ In a wide shallow frying pan, fry garlic gently in a little olive oil until the aroma rises. Add tin of tomatoes, sugar, a little salt and pepper, and basil or mint. Cook vigorously to reduce.

+ Brush shallow, oven-proof, ceramic dish with a little olive oil. Arrange slices of eggplant to cover the bottom, overlapping a little.

+ Cover with the tomato sauce, spread over the diced mozzarella or cottage cheese, and top with grated parmesan and bake for 30 minutes.

Antico risotto sabaudo – Risotto with ham and cheese

Another Claudia Roden recipe, this comes from Italy's Piedmont/
Valle d'Aosta region. It was one of the first things I made for myself
after Harvey died. It's such comforting food, like savoury rice
pudding. Surprisingly, it freezes well too. Roden says jellied meat
juice is an optional addition at the end. So is sliced white truffle,
but that's never come my way. This is good with a tomato and basil
salad, or with asparagus. Serves 4–6.

> 50g butter
> 1 medium onion, finely chopped
> 100g cooked ham, preferably in a piece or thick slices,
>   then cubed (more than Roden uses)
> 1 large sprig rosemary
> 400g Arborio rice
> 150ml white wine
> 1.25l chicken stock, heated
> 150–200g fontina or gruyère cheese, diced (again, more
>   than Roden uses)
> 4–6 tablespoons freshly grated parmesan cheese

- Melt the butter over low heat in a saucepan, add onion and cook
  gently for 5 minutes until soft but not coloured.

- Add ham and cook for 1 minute, then add rosemary and rice,
  stirring until rice is transparent. (Mine never seems to go fully
  transparent, but this does not matter.)

- Add wine, then stir and cook until absorbed. Add hot stock a
  ladleful at a time, stirring until each is absorbed. After about 20
  minutes, rice should be creamy but still a little al dente.

- Stir in fontina or gruyère cheese and cook for another 5 minutes.

- Serve in warmed pasta plates with parmesan scattered over the top.

Books that have inspired me

Memoirs

Julian Barnes, *The Pedant in the Kitchen*: Atlantic Books, 2003

Julia Child and Alex Prud'homme, *My Life in France*: Alfred A. Knopf, 2006

Elizabeth David, *An Omelette and a Glass of Wine*: Penguin, 1984

Elizabeth David and Jill Norman, *Is There a Nutmeg in the House?*: Viking, 2001

M.F.K. Fisher, *As They Were*: Vintage Books, 1983

M.F.K. Fisher, *The Art of Eating*: Wiley Publishing, 1990

Amanda Hesser (ed.), *Eat, Memory: Great Writers at the Table*, (A collection of essays from the *New York Times*): W.W. Norton & Co., 2008

Shonagh Koea, *The Kindness of Strangers: Kitchen Memoirs*: Random House, 2007

Harvey McQueen, *This Piece of Earth: A Life in My New Zealand Garden*: Awa Press, 2004 (now available as ebook only)

Ruth Reichl, *Tender at the Bone: Growing Up at the Table*: Random House, 1998

Ruth Reichl, *Comfort Me with Apples: More Adventures at the Table*: Random House, 2001

Nigel Slater, *Toast: The Story of a Boy's Hunger*: Fourth Estate, 2003

Recipe books

Stephanie Alexander, *Cooking and Travelling in South-West France*: Viking, 2002

Ada Boni, *The Talisman Italian Cookbook*: Crown Publishers, 1950

Dean Brettschneider, *Pie*: Penguin, 2012

Julia Child, Louisette Bertholle and Simone Beck, *Mastering the Art of French Cooking, Volume I*: Alfred A. Knopf, 1961

Lois Daish, *A Good Year*: Random House, 2005

Elizabeth David, *French Provincial Cooking*: Michael Joseph, 1960

Richard Ehrlich, *The Lazy Cook: Simple, Sophisticated Food and How to Make it*: Bantam, 1993

Rosemary Hume and Muriel Downes, *Cordon Bleu Desserts and Puddings*: Penguin, 1975

Digby Law, *A Soup Cookbook*: Hodder and Stoughton, 1982

Digby Law, *A Vegetable Cookbook*: Hodder and Stoughton, 1978

Judith Olney, *The Joy of Chocolate*: Barron's Educational Series, 1982

Claudia Roden, *A Book of Middle Eastern Food*: Penguin, 1968; also *The New Book of Middle Eastern Food*: Alfred A. Knopf, 2000

Claudia Roden, *The Food of Italy*: Chatto & Windus, 1989 also *The Food of Italy: Region by Region*: Steerforth Italia, 2003

Nancy Spain, *The Nancy Spain Colour Cookery Book*: World Distributors, 1963

Patricia Wells and Joël Robuchon, *Cuisine Actuelle*: Macmillan, 1993; US edition *Simply French*: Hearst Books, 1995

Katharine Whitehorn, *Cooking in a Bedsitter*: Penguin, 1963